Total Life Pursuit

Total Life Pursuit

Living Remarkably in the Six Major Areas of Life

TERRY MILLER

Requests for information or orders contact:
Miller Tribe Publishing, 3303 Harbor Blvd, Costa Mesa, CA 92626 or 714.435.1400

www.TotalLifePursuit.org

First edition: October 2013

ISBN-13: 978-0-9912579-0-4

This book is dedicated to

those who want to get to the next level of living,
those who deem mediocre is not enough, and to
those who want the struggle with no results to end.
It is to the young, the old and all of those in between
who desire to live remarkably
in *every* area of life.

Contents

Preface

The older I get the more I pay attention to life's lessons. Being over 50 has its advantages, but it has its disadvantages too! My knowledge and wisdom have tripled or quadrupled since my early adult years (hopefully more than that), but so has the effort it takes to do certain things. I have tried to learn from others in life so I don't have to suffer from the same mistakes. I watched my mom deteriorate from a vibrant woman to someone who couldn't get around anymore. The cause was inactivity, poor diet and alcoholism along with her pessimistic thinking and a few other things. I swore that I wouldn't end my life living that way.

I remember after my very strong do-it-yourself father-in-law had his first stroke (that was some time after open heart surgery), he said to me, "If you don't slow down you will end up being slowed down by your body just like me." That was a wakeup call! I can't remember how many kids I had at that time (I have eight now)...it might have been right after number seven, but who is counting. I had started a church and I owned my own business and I worked for this other guy a little on the side. I was burning the candle at both ends. You are probably guessing that I am a Type A personality, a go-getter, a "Get 'er done" sort of guy—well, you would be right.

When I was in Junior High School I started taking anti-depressants for what is now called IBS (irritable bowel syndrome). I was unaware that they were treating me for depression, but that didn't slow me down much, although I suffered pain every day. If I were in school today, I would be on Ritalin or something like it because I was hyper. Now let's fast-forward to my adult years where I epitomize a hyper, Type A individual. I was driven to succeed because of some perfectionist tendencies; and because my wife and I kept having kids and decided to live in Southern California (where living is expensive) I was burning out and stressing out, but I didn't know it. I have had numerous stress diseases such as IBS, muscle spasms and cramping (mainly in my back), and that last one (several years ago), heart arrhythmia. That one is the most fun! I have prayed that I wouldn't die...several times, but I now know that it was all about my stress levels and how I lived life.

I have always stressed out about money, and one day about seven or eight years ago I heard the voice of God (so tangible that it was nearly audible), after I was saying something like, "I'll never have enough money to get out of debt and buy a home." God said to me, "I can't do anything with an attitude like that." That was another marker, a learning experience like the ones mentioned above. I have experienced them in my marriage, my finances, my parenting, my emotional life (mainly stress), my mental life, my physical life and even my spiritual life.

I have other life experiences, the results of which compelled me to do research and to focus on changing my own life so I can live with greatness, excellence or whatever you want to name. I was tired of being mediocre and stressed out! I wanted to enjoy life, and I wanted to enjoy it well into my 80s. After all, I am the life-of-the-party type of guy. I love to have fun, laugh and enjoy life! I do enjoy life, except when I am all stressed out! I looked around at most 70 and 80 year olds and they weren't enjoying some aspect of their lives—whether physical, mental, emotional, spiritual, relational or financial, or all or most of them. I didn't want to be like them, so I changed!

Introduction

As a pastor for the last 18 years, I have been in the people business. I see a lot of people and walk with them through life and see the need to help them excel in every area of their lives, not just the spiritual. I saw a disconnect between the spiritual aspect of life and the other aspects, not a total disconnect, but enough to cause some alarms to go off. I saw it in others and I saw it in myself, so I made some choices that have changed my life forever. Now I am writing and speaking a message of hope into others: your life is meant to be great and you can live it that way!

Moses was 120 years old when he died. The Bible says that he was full of strength (and his eyes had not failed) when he died. That is going to be me! (Not the 120 years, but the part about dying full of strength). We all will die, but how long will we be dying? In my 80s, I will not be forgetting where I put my keys or what I had for breakfast. I will not be stressed and my marriage will still rock all the more. I will not need to depend on the government for my retirement, and I will still be able to surf and ride my road bike 50 miles whenever I want to! Really, my greatest aspiration is to know God more and bring Him more glory with the way I live my life—totally. I don't want a mediocre life or a couple parts of my life to be good, I want Total Life!

In my youth and young adulthood (and even now), I could play every sport. Granted I wasn't great in any particular sport, but I could hold my own in a pick-up game with the average Joe. There is a phrase for that, "jack of all trades and master of none." I guess it crossed over into my adult life in all areas of life and didn't stay compartmentalized into sports. I like excelling, I love winning, but honestly I don't want to put the time in to be the best or even to be great at any one thing. I think that is a picture of most of the West and maybe even the world. We have become content with "getting through," with "making it," with "surviving." I have another name for it—mediocre!

Jesus Christ said this very bold statement, "The thief comes only to steal and kill and destroy. I have come that they may have life and have it abundantly." (John 10:10 ESV) If you have been around church for any amount of time, you have heard this, but do you really understand what He is saying? I suppose some would say that He meant eternal life—I agree. In fact, eternal life starts now. If that is right, then what kind of life does He want you to have today? Abundant life! What is that? One thing is for sure: it is not a mediocre life!

Abundant comes from the Greek word perissos, which means super abundant, over and above, beyond measure (in quantity), and superior (in quality). Any way you slice this, it means that we are supposed to live far beyond so-so or hanging in there or any other forms of mediocre. Jesus said, "I have come that" or, "I have come [in order] that...[we] might have..." One of the reasons that Jesus came to Earth was to give us the opportunity to live a life that is great in every aspect, a life that is super abundant and superior! If that is what He said, then that is what He has given to us.

I will go into this verse a bit more in the first chapter, but we need to see one more thing here: Jesus said that we "might" have it. That makes you think, huh? Maybe if you were born in a good place or you are from a good family you could have it. Maybe if you had some good schooling or good coaches who gave you more than sporting or academic instruction you would get it. Maybe.... The maybe is this: if you take hold of it, and choose to go after it, and you choose to receive it when it is right there in front of you, then you will have it! We must not be lulled into thinking that if God wants you to have abundant life then he will hand-deliver it with a red bow on top and a message saying, "To: You—From: Your Heavenly Father." I will admit that God has dropped things in my lap just like that. There was that time that my friend Poi called me out of the blue and told me that God told him to shape me and give me a surfboard! That was awesome! However, God didn't give me any more ability to surf, He just gave me the tool to shred (that is surfer lingo for doing well). So do I shred now, about 10 years later? No, I just surf; my kids can shred though! I will tell you what I did do with that tool; I used it how it was intended. It gave me hours of enjoyment and exercise, time with my kids, time with God, relaxation and recreation. I used that tool to the max (another surfing phrase meaning going all the way), and I need another board! (Poi, dawg, how about it?)

Life has six major areas: spiritual, mental, emotional, physical, relational and financial. They are all very close connected to each other. Most of us have one or two going pretty well and, if you are on top of things, three areas mastered. What I mean by mastered is that you believe, and others around you would concur, that you are living beyond the normal and nowhere near mediocre. You realize that you still need improvement, there is plenty of headroom for you, but you are excelling and accelerating in those areas. You put forth great effort to move up to the next level and you haven't settled for the level you are on yet. That is great! (Really!) Still, there are three, four or five other areas that need your attention.

As a Christ-follower, the one area of my life in which I haven't settled for "so-so-ness" is my relationship with God. I am passionate about knowing Him, serving Him, leading people towards Him and experiencing Him. I have been in ministry for decades (about three), and I have seen many people who are more "religious" than "relational" in regard to God. Yet with both groups there is some kind of disconnect between our spiritual life and the rest of the areas of life. That is just plain weird! I understand not having the tools to better yourself, but to be able to separate your relationship with God out and disconnect it is, well, strange! In philosophy that school of thought could be called Platonic Dualism, which spawned a few other groups who believed that the spiritual and the physical were separate and not connected. So basically you could do whatever you wanted with your body, and it would not matter in your spiritual life. Lame!

The East (eastern religion) has been saying we are holistic, interconnected beings, and they are right! However, they didn't come up with that thought, it is all throughout the Bible. Paul writes to the Thessalonians, "May your whole spirit, soul and body be kept blameless at the coming of our Lord Jesus Christ." (1 Thes 5:23) We are tied together no matter how you slice us! When we think a certain way we will attach an emotion to the thought, which affects us physically (whether good or bad—more on that later), which will in turn affect our relationships, including our relationship with God. How we choose to live, to operate, our chosen pattern of living and way of life is going to affect all of us. We cannot compartmentalize different areas into closets in our hearts, brains or bodies. They are all connected!

There are people who are floaters. Those are people who float through life. They go where life takes them. Really, they are victims in most areas of life. Picture a raft filled with a family on a river. The family is having lunch and enjoying the beauty of nature. They are laughing and having all kinds of fun. Then it happens —rapids. (Rapids have a 1-5 rating, 5 being the kind of rapids in which you fear for your life and had better have the skills to navigate.) Ahead of the family is a Level 2 rapid. So there are some bumps and their drinks get spilled, but they come through it well enough. They don't really enjoy it because they were having lunch and it interrupted their intentions, but they get back to lunch. Ahead of them there is a fork in the river. To the right are Level 5 rapids and to the left are more Level 2 rapids, but mostly calm water. What would you do? You have your ten-year-old, your four-year-old, your one-year-old and your spouse with you. You would pick the left fork—correct? So many people just go wherever the river takes them. We don't think about the future and what it may hold, they just go with the flow. Once we encounter the Level 5 rapids we wish we would have scouted ahead to make a better choice, but it is too late. Now we must face them and we aren't prepared. Not only do we wish we would have chosen the left fork, but we also wish we had trained for the Level 5 rapids. We wish we would have taken classes, gotten in shape or even had a faith-filled relationship with God so that at least you would have confidence in your prayers. But it is too late; now you have to face your choices. I want you to decide right now whether you will be a floater, or whether you will be a guide that navigates the boat where you want. Here is the cool thing: if you have survived Level 5 rapids there is still time to be trained as a guide. It is never too late!

What follows is a book of encouragement and information to help you make the swap from mediocre to excellent, from so-so to extraordinary, from just making it to super abundant. You will receive practical advice and thought provoking information in each of the six areas of life with how-to sections to get to the next level. The how to sections may not be specific to your circumstance, but they are principles, and if they are applied, they will propel you to greater things and a life that is lived on a higher level. You will embark on a journey of mastery. Just imagine being able to master your schedule! That should bring a smile to your face. It is possible! Picture yourself physically healthy in your 80s and 90s. You are mentally sharp, emotionally balanced, in good physical health and financially sound, with many meaningful relationships, including a close connection to God. The possibilities that God has given us within our mind, body and soul are amazing! Our potential is untapped by most!

The Bible says, "…all things are possible to him who believes." (Mark 9:23 NASB) I believe that! This book is about more than human potential, which is better than we realize, yet our own human potential pales when compared to the ability that God gives us. "With God all things are possible." (Matthew 19:26) He is for you, with you, and wants you to excel. Renewing your mind, living with peace, and staying vibrant and healthy are not pie-in-the-sky dreams; they are the dreams of our Creator for us. With God's strength and wisdom, you can do all things!

I can tell you that taking care of yourself and living in super abundance is worth the effort that it takes to get there. None of us want to diminish mentally, we don't want to let stress ravage our minds and bodies, or have a failed or horrible marriage, or use a walker to get around in our 70s. We all want to be vibrant, full of life, sharp as a tack and have the wisdom of Solomon! We want to be able to retire from our primary career without the worry of being homeless or hungry. We all want to live what we have dreamed of…. What I am telling you is that you can if you pursue it! So, get buckled up and enjoy the journey, because it is going to take you where you have only dreamed of being before today.

1

You Can Change

Change is Inevitable

One way or another, things change in life. Whether it is your age, your balance sheet, or the oil in your car, things change. Most things change whether you want them to or not. The question is: do you let things change with or without your influence? Let's take getting older for example. Everyone but Benjamin Button gets older. However, you can determine *how* you are going to get older. You can either get older and physically decay at the normal rate for the West, and spend 10-25 years wishing things were different because you can't move around well (and all the other things that can come with decaying), or you can be proactive and make the change work for you. Decrepitness is not a foregone conclusion. The "over the hill" concept is wrong from the outset. You can slow, and even stop the decay of your body, and in many ways even reverse that decay.

Your body is an amazing creation of God! You have a say in how you age. Let's take an example of the oil in your car engine. You can change it every 3,000-5,000 miles, or you can change it every 20,000 miles. However, your engine will show the difference in its longevity. In other words, when you influence the change with wisdom, there is a better outcome. You have something to do with it. Similarly, you can plan for a better financial future, ensure a fantastic and lengthy marriage, and know where your car keys are at all times if you intentionally influence the changes in your life.

There are other things (far fewer), that won't change unless you determine yourself to enact the change. If you make meatloaf the same way every Monday night, it will be the same meatloaf you have cooked for the last 20 years unless you determine to change your recipe, cooking time, or temperature. Whether it should change or not, it will only change with effort. Like most things the meatloaf recipe won't change on its own, you have to change it. In the same way, your attitude toward certain things won't change unless you cognitively make the change. You have to determine to change or your thinking will stay the same about certain things. Again, there are things that may not need to change, but if they do only you can make the change.

Most things will fall into the second law of thermodynamics category (the law of entropy). Simply put: things run down. For example, the universe is spreading out, ice melts in a warm room, and the energy in batteries doesn't last forever. This law affects us in every area of our lives. Have you ever known a negative and crabby thirty-something? Were you able to see them in their sixties? They were crabbier! We all have to push against the law of entropy, just like we do when we preserve our cars' paint with some good wax. Eventually a car will need a new paint job; however, the difference in how long the paint lasts with and without care will be in years. If we want our car's paint to look great for 10-20 years, then we have to put the effort in to stem the tide of degeneration. The same reasoning applies to all of our lives. For example, if you don't put effort into your marriage, you may stay married, but you won't have people asking you for marital advice. Your marriage will be at best mediocre. So with all this, is there any hope? Oh, yes! We are fearfully and wonderfully made.

Why You Need to Take Control of the Change

Imagine you are going to a terrific five-star getaway with your spouse in a secluded cabin in a beautiful forest. It has an amazing view; it is wonderfully appointed, and has a full-size hot tub in the bedroom. The refrigerator has been stocked for you, and it is yours for a three-night romantic getaway. It has everything a couple could want including a great sound system, a pool table, and even a 72-inch big screen television with a prepaid chick-flick. (Okay, so if it were a man's dream there would be sports on the screen, but for the love of the wife, it has her movie choice.) Imagine it has been some time since you and your spouse have done anything like this; in fact, it has been years. Let's say you are going down a windy road, and you are about to have to cross a bridge to get to the fabulous cabin. All of a sudden you see a sign, "Bridge out." What do you do? Do you keep going as if you didn't see the sign? That is a bad idea, right? Maybe you proceed with great caution and take a look for yourself. Whatever you do you are going to have to change your route, right? Next, you learn that the bridge is indeed out. Now what? You want to get to that cabin. Four days and three nights with your honey in a fantastic place—it is just what your marriage needs to get it kick-started again. The romance has been lacking for some time now and you know you really need to reconnect. So what do you do? You find a way to get there! You do whatever it takes, right? What if you have to drive an extra two hours? Would you just turn around and go home, or do you "Get 'er done?" I have a feeling that if you were anything like me, you would carry the luggage and hike to the cabin if you had to. You would pay whatever price you could to get to the cabin. Once you got there, you would be glad that you made the choice to make the effort. The reward is waiting for you.

In life, just like in the illustration of getting to the cabin, there are wonderful blessings that await you. Things that you yourself have wanted, and that you admit you need. Sometimes, however, maybe even most of the time, those things don't just appear in your lap, in your bank account, or on the kitchen table. You have to go get them. You have to make the choice, make the effort, and use your strength and ability to attain them—and they are attainable!

In Order to Change, You Must Believe the Need to Change is Necessary

The fact that we must believe change is necessary may seem like an understatement, or something that everyone understands, but this is the first thing we need to accept. We need change! Our thought patterns in regard to change being necessary need to be recognized and evaluated. There is this way of thinking that we have already arrived at the place we should be. It's the thought that we have already mastered an area of life and we need to go no further. Can you imagine saying that? I can't either, yet there are times that we must believe something like that, because we see no need to change as if we have attained all that there is to attain. I remember my very wise father-in-law saying something in his late 60s like, "You would think that after all these years of walking with God, and the life that I have lived with all of its lessons, that I wouldn't have to keep learning these lessons, but I guess I do." He was a wise man indeed because he was very aware of his shortcomings, and that is the first step of change: we have to see the need for it. Have we been duped into thinking that we are already *good enough*? Most people would not say that about themselves; however, we all may think it from time to time. Take an inventory right now—get honest.

Is there room for improvement in you spiritual life? Do you have the relationship with God that you have dreamed of? Do you follow your beliefs and convictions? Do you live according to/up to your morals? Does what you believe about God affect the other areas of your life?

How is your thinking and mental agility? Are you as sharp as you used to be? Do you have negative thinking circuits that are hard to control? Are you in control of what you think and how long you will think about it?

How is your management of stress and deadly emotions (hatred, bitterness, malice...)? Do you find yourself stressed out on a regular basis, or even daily? Does stress affect other parts of your life? Do you struggle with forgiveness or get offended easily? Does your day "get away from you" on a regular basis? Are you generally happy and great to be around?

Think about your relationships, your close ones: could you improve on them? Is your marriage great? Does your spouse think your marriage is great? Are you able to love unencumbered? Do you think about how to build and strengthen relationships with others?

Could you have your finances more in order, or could you be in more control of your finances? Have you settled for always struggling or just getting by? Are you in debt up to your eyeballs and have no clue how to escape? Do you believe that you could be a supplier for charities in a big way?

Finally, how is your health and fitness? Are you aging gracefully or declining quickly? If you walked up two flights of stairs would you be out of breath? Could you sit up in your bed without the use of your arms to pull you up? Are you sick often? Do you lack energy during the day? Do you eat what your body needs instead of what you want?

Well, how did you do? Did you just read through or did you stop and give yourself a real assessment? What did you come up with? What areas need some change? If you are like me, your answer is, "All of them!" Don't get discouraged by that answer. The "all of them" answer is actually a great indicator of your truthful assessment of your life. That is the mindset that you want. That is the first step. You have to admit that you need the change, or at least that there is room for change. Even if you need to improve on an area of strength, something that you are doing well in life, there is always room to get to the next level.

I look at life like a stairway. Every step leads you either higher or lower or you are marching in place. When I talk about elevating to the next level of living, I am talking about elevating the way you operate your life. For instance, if your finances are in an unknown state of bad, your first level is to get a handle on what you are spending and what your necessary expenses are every month. The next level is to set up a spending plan. The next level is to spend only what you have planned. I think you get the point. Believe it or not, there are many levels still to be attained within the realm of finances. We have only scratched the surface.

What is your greatest area of need? Is there another level in any of the six areas that you need to achieve? Make a deal with yourself right now that you are going to be bluntly honest and leave no stone unturned in your assessment of your life. If you find it difficult, ask your spouse, kids or parents to be bluntly honest in helping you assess your life. This isn't necessarily about what areas in your life would be considered bad, but instead which areas could use some improvement. I'll tell you truthfully, there isn't an area in my life in which I wouldn't want to see some level of improvement. I want to grow and get to the next level in every area of life.

5

In Order to Change, You Have to Believe the Effort You Make is Going to Pay Off

Let's go back to the illustration in which the bridge is washed out. If you think you are going to have an awful time with your spouse, then you would use the bridge as an excuse to turn around and go home. You would want to just leave things as they are instead of making an effort to change. However, if you think that your marriage would be changed, and you want it changed, you would do whatever you need to do to get there. In life, the same thinking applies with Bible reading, scheduling your days, working out, or anything else you want improvement in—if you think it is worth the effort, time, money, and energy then you will be more likely to make the change. As you read this book, you will see that the effort pays great dividends, and is totally worth it!

In Order to Change You Have to Believe Change is Possible

Another type of thinking that needs to be recognized is that you are stuck with the cards that you are dealt. For example, you have a hand, (in Texas hold 'em) of an off-suited two and six and the flop hasn't helped you. In life, that thinking may look like this: after all, you only make so much money so how could your finances improve, right? Wrong! The possibilities for growth in every area of your life are endless. Do you remember playing poker as kids? (Some of you never did, I know, it's *gambling*; I gambled with candy—which my parents wanted me to lose!) My friends and I would deal seven cards to each other and then we would turn some cards back in for new cards. We have the option to do some trading in life. The difference is that in life, we pick the cards that are given to us a second time instead of receiving them by chance as in my youthful poker game.

Some would say that I have always been an angry person; I have the Irish/Italian/German…temper. (It is funny how just about every country is known for short-tempered people.) I might think, "I have always been like this; it's just who I am." That is some stinkin' thinkin' and an excuse to avoid change. Others would say that I have always been forgetful, clumsy, overweight, sickly…and the list goes on.

There is hope! The hope that I have is much more than the hope in buying a lottery ticket and *wishing* I would win. My hope is a confident expectation of success.

We have such potential that God has engineered into our beings. We sell ourselves so short! No champion thinks, "Well, I failed before; I'll probably be stuck in a cycle of failings." Thomas Edison tried 1,000 experiments before he invented the commercial incandescent light bulb. He was considered a misfit and stopped formal education at age twelve. He was partially deaf and hated rote work. He was too imaginative and might have been diagnosed with ADD. He holds more patents (159) than any other person in history. Whatever his hindrances or heritage (three of his siblings died—he was the youngest of seven children), whatever cards he was dealt, he was determined to unleash the gifts inside of himself and fulfill his destiny. He wasn't satisfied with one or two inventions or even twelve; he just kept going. There is a similarity between Edison, and you, and myself: we are all human, with great God-endowed potential. We have the power to change the shape of our brains for goodness-sake just by thinking! (More on that in the Mental Part of the Whole chapter.) We can change. God has created a magnificent person, you—and if you would stop the thinking that has kept you where you are, held you back, or has infinitely slowed your progress in life to a crawl, you would burst from where you are into where you are destined to be!

We each have a destiny, a calling from our Creator Himself. We were designed to do many things and to be great at them. We each have a specific destiny. So many people are afraid to believe that they have a destiny, let alone think about what it may be. You were created for purpose. You are significant. You can rise above wherever you are right now in life, whether you are doing so-so, well, or horribly. You can, you must, fulfill the destiny that God has given you!

Because of the bad things that happen to us, the difficulties that we experience, or the difficult things we watch others go through, we doubt that God's plan for us is good. If we are honest, most of us can believe God has a great plan for others, but when it comes to us, well, that is a different story. In the introduction I mentioned a particular verse located in John 10:10, "The thief comes only to steal and kill and destroy; I [Jesus] have come that they may have life, and have it to the full." The New Living Translation (NLT) puts it like this, "The thief's purpose is to steal and kill and destroy. My purpose is to give them a rich and satisfying life." Are you getting this? God's design and will for you is to abound, to have fullness, to live life in super abundance. I could quote another 50 verses, but this one should suffice to show you God's design and will for your life. God wants us to have great lives! Not lives without trouble, not lives without any suffering (trouble and suffering are a part of life), but through it all we will have lives lived in fullness, not in emptiness, and certainly not mediocre lives.

There is an important point here that must not be missed. This verse is talking about sheep inside God's sheep pen. This sheep pen is where you can fulfill your maximum purpose, your maximum destiny: with God. If you are outside, come on in, and enjoy the benefits of everlasting life and maximum fullness in this life. At the end of this book I describe a relationship with Jesus, the Christ. If you aren't sure whether you are in His sheep pen, then go to the back of the book and make sure, because there you will find great news for His sheep. Not only do we all have God-given potential do to amazing things, but God has strength that He is willing to give to those who are committed to Him. Think about it. God energizes you with His ability and strength—now that is amazing!

The Enemy of Change for the Better

In the Introduction I talked about living life to the full and the principle of "might" (we "might" have abundant life), which tells us that we have the possibility of this type of life and not the certainty. There is the possibility of us not having the life that God wants for us! It is our choice and honestly, it is our battle. It is worth fighting for. Let me focus in on something so many have missed—life is not just an adventure, it is a battle. Not only do you have to battle your own tendencies to stop short of your destiny, but there is a person, a power, an evil that wants to rip you off! The thief wants you to believe that God doesn't want you to live life to the full; he wants you to settle for half-full, or even empty. There is a personal devil whose job is to confound us by the terrible things that go on around us, the horrible things people have proclaimed over us, the circumstances from which we seemingly can never get out from under, and a few hundred other ploys. If, in fact, we believe that we have received a rotten lot in life and we can do nothing to change, he has done his job and all of hell is cheering and laughing at us. Hell, at its very base level, is the absence of God and everything that is good. Has hell gotten a hold on your belief system? Is God absent, or has he been hamstrung or made impotent? The thief's purpose is to make you impotent. There should be something rising up within you right now saying—*no way!* Giving away your destiny to the forces of hell is like a 10-year-old who came up to you with a water pistol and demanded your wallet. Would you give it to him? No way! Then don't give away your destiny to someone far inferior to you. We wouldn't fear a water pistol and we should not fear the devil, failure or anything else.

The fear of failure stops us from trying. It keeps us from attaining things that we are not sure we could attain if we tried. For example, many marriages suffer divorce simply because one or both spouses are afraid they won't measure up, so they just give up. Little do they know that they are going to have to put an incredible amount of energy and resource into a divorce—more than they ever dreamed. The point is that you will never know if you could have done something if you don't try.

I remember my children didn't like certain foods as they were growing up. I am sure we were the same way when we were kids. However, there comes a point where our tastes change and suddenly what we didn't like before, we like now. It is as if something happened to the peas or avocado that makes you think it is good now. The same type of thing is possible in life. There are things that we have failed in or are currently failing at that are ripe for a breakthrough. This may be our time to master it. For example, in my life, I tried for years to work with a schedule and dismally failed. Now I feel naked without a schedule and on the days that I ignore it, I get very little done. What once was my enemy has now become my close friend. It is time to give those things that you have failed at before another shot. You are different now. You have matured and gained wisdom. Do it!

If you invented four devices and only one of them sold, would you be happy? If you played baseball and got on base one out of every three times, would you be satisfied? I know a guy who just graduated from a police academy. Many agencies were interviewing him because he was near the top of his class (plus, he is tall and muscular). There were half a dozen agencies where he wanted to work. Do you think he was happy when one of those six offered him a job even though the others turned him down? Of course he was happy. It meant that all the effort and intense training that he put himself through paid off. The other five agencies didn't matter when his focus was success. Now let's suppose that he was afraid he wouldn't be hired by any agency; would he have even gone through the academy? No.

I heard about a factory worker that waited over 20 years to get promoted to management. He went from blue collar to white collar, which substantially increased his salary. Instead of going to the factory the Monday after his promotion, he had to cross a river and go to the corporate offices. When he saw what he was going to have to do as a manager he was afraid that he wouldn't make it. He didn't think that he had what it took. His bosses thought he did, but he didn't. He was afraid of failing. Suddenly he developed a fear of bridges. He saw a psychologist who couldn't help him overcome his fear of bridges. This meant that he couldn't cross that bridge to get to his new position, the one he had wanted for two decades. Because of his newfound fear of bridges, he went back to work in the factory and gave up the promotion. He wasn't afraid of bridges: he was afraid of failure. So that which he always wanted, he gave up because he was afraid.

The Bible says that, "God has not given us a spirit of fear, but of power and of love and of a sound mind." (2 Timothy 1:7 NKJV) We can overcome fear of failure with God's help and a decision that we are not going to be beat. We have to first decide that it is possible, and then we have to decide that the effort is worth it. Yet there is something that we tend to struggle with, and that is we don't think we deserve it.

Some settle for so-so, mediocre lives because that's all they think they are worth. After all, they have messed things up, they have divorced, they have allowed themselves to get completely out of shape, and the list goes on. They figure that because they caused it they deserve their lot in life and that is where they should stay. That sounds more like Hinduism and the cast system which teaches that your lot in this life is because of what you have done in your past life! That is not what God says about life or about you. You have to decide, right now, whether you value what God says about you over what you think about yourself.

Jeremiah 29:11 says, "'For I know the plans I have for you,' declares the Lord, 'plans to prosper you and not to harm you, plans to give you hope and a future.'" This was written during a time of punishment for Israel: they were in exile. God told them not to listen to the bad news prophets, the ones who were saying that God didn't care, that He was so angry that it was over for them—that this was their lot. No, God told them to plant gardens where they were, and pray for their city to prosper so they would prosper as well. Then He told them that He would bring them back to their land, and that if they sought Him, they would find Him. That was incredible! Right in the middle of all of that, He told them that His plan is to prosper them; it always had been and always would be. He has a destiny for all to reach and He has a plan to get you there too. We have the same type of bad news prophets today. They tell us that God doesn't want to prosper us, but the Bible says that He does. Now don't just think money when you hear the word prosper: think marriage, children, your body, mind, and soul as well. Don't even say to yourself that God doesn't want you to achieve more, because He does. He wants you to live on such a level that everyone will say, "Well, it must be God working in his or her life, because he or she just couldn't do that alone!"

I hope that by now you can see that God is for you, and wants you to reach higher and higher levels of living in every area of your life. I could write a whole book about the way God feels and thinks about you. Do you know that you are His daily delight? Well you are! It is time for us to start lining up our opinions of ourselves with God's opinion of us. It isn't like He doesn't see all the crud, all the failings, all the moral failures; but even though He knows these things, He sees the beauty of who we are and what we can be. It's like a man who said to his friend, "Look at this forest. What do you see?" The friend said, "I see trees and lots of them. Why? What do you see?" The man said, "I see houses, tables, chairs, baseball bats and Lincoln Log sets." God sees you for what you will be. Will you begin to look into the future (even if it is a month from now), and see the possibilities?

The Mechanics of Change

I am no physicist (I couldn't even spell the word without a spellchecker), but I do understand motion. It takes more energy to get something into motion than it does to keep it in motion, and it takes more energy to stop something that is already in motion than it does to keep it in motion. In other words, starting something is a lot harder than maintaining it. Stopping something is akin to starting something. If you are used to having desert every night, and you decide that eating carbs at bedtime is a bad idea (which it is), it is going to take a lot more energy to stop than to keep having that pazooki (a huge, deep-dish, warmed cookie covered in ice cream).

So let's take a look at some of the mechanics of change.

Being Honest—Seeing the Need

We first must have an honest evaluation of where we are and where we want to be. As stated before, there will be no positive change that propels one to greater living if one doesn't think he or she needs it.

Heeding Instruction

The Proverbs are replete with the thought of the wise heeding instruction and of the foolish scorning it. It cannot be stated more deftly than it is in the Proverbs. If we didn't need instruction, then we would be God. As far as I can tell, He is the only one who doesn't need help getting to the next level of living in any area. We, however, are fortunate to have so many fantastic resources to help us, instruct us, embolden us and encourage us to get to that next level of living.

Just as bad as the floater mentality mentioned before is the island mentality: "I am an island unto myself." This is a destructive type of thinking that will hold you back from greatness, and even from mediocrity. Even Tiger Woods has a coach. Do you think that his coach could play golf as well as he can? Nope! He is a coach, not a player. I am sure he could beat you and me for sure, but that is not his role. His role is to instruct, and Tiger's role is to heed the instruction. I will talk about our need for connectedness in a later chapter, but suffice it to say that if you don't heed the instruction of the wise, you are a fool.

Correct Thinking

We need to have correct and positive thinking. Long ago I learned in counseling classes that proper feelings come from proper behavior, which comes from proper thinking. I have seen this demonstrated time and time again, just as you and many others have as well. The way we think determines how we behave and feel. Most of this thinking is at the core of our belief system and is sometimes hidden from a surface view. However, all thinking starts as a willful act. Even when we were too young to realize that what others said about us was a lie and a distortion of the truth, we willfully accepted it. Thinking is the starting place for change, and it cannot be overstated. We have to believe we have the capacity to change to make the changes we want to make. Our minds need renewal in many areas. That is what makes me so excited about this book and subsequent *Total Life Pursuit* courses—your thinking is going to change, and so is everything else! You must believe that you need change, that you are worth the change, and that you can change, or you will only change for the worse.

Strength, Determination and Effort

I think about all of the fad diets that have come and gone. The most popular ones are the ones that say, "Take this pill and look like a full-sized Barbie doll." The promised results take zero effort, except the effort it takes to pay for the magic pill. They don't work, do they? It is like the theory of osmosis, that we could learn while sleeping by getting a book on tape and playing it during sleep. Really? Would you expect to pass the test on that book? Probably not, but you probably wish it was true.

Whatever we do, whether it is cooking food so we can eat, or taking the trash out so it isn't stinking up our houses, it takes effort. If you are married, how much effort did you put into dating, courting and marrying your spouse? You put in a whole bunch of effort, right? Why do we think that it will take very little effort to have a great marriage? It takes effort to spend all the money you have but it takes greater effort to put yourself on a spending plan and exercise restraint. To be great, to have the life you've always dreamed of, you have to exert effort.

Your life has certain inertia, and if you are going to change, it will take more effort to change than to remain the same. It takes more energy to begin motion than it does to continue motion. It takes more energy to go against the flow of life or your usual pattern of thinking and behavior than it does to stay the same. Change is going to take effort. You will have to use energy and more of it in order to change. You will need to be determined to use your strength to affect something different in your life. Whether you are going to have to stop doing something, or start doing something, or pull a complete U-turn, it is going to take effort. In real life this can be painful. We in the West are not so used to pain, or having to wait for that matter. We are quickly becoming a people who would rather suck off the nipple of someone else's bottle than buy our own cow, milk her ourselves, bottle it and drink it out of our own cups. To excel at anything takes personal responsibility and requisitioning the strength within you. The good news is that you have the strength and determination that it takes!

Power to Change

There are three main things that it will take to make changes in your life, to live above your current existence. They are effort, strength and choice. First of all, you have to choose it, every day. Let's say you are 25 pounds overweight. (That is overweight according to what you know to be a realistic weight, not some government data sheet.) If I ask how you got there, you may answer something like, "one pound at a time." While that is true, here is the more accurate statement: "one decision after another." How would you lose that weight? You would lose the weight one pound at a time, right? How would you lose one pound? You would lose one pound with one choice after another.

Our creator has endowed us with the ability to choose. You can be an atheist and still believe you have the power of choice. It is this power of choice that will determine the outcome of our lives, which means that the ball is in our courts. By admitting that you have a choice in the matter, you rise above victim status and you are already on your way to your next level. Choice is a magnificent power. Other definitions of choice are volition, or will. When I use the word will, the word *willpower* comes to mind (and some of you just started to go down a bad road by thinking that is what you lack). No you don't! You have the willpower to change.

Victim status is playing the victim. You know these people and if we are honest, we can act like that to one degree or another ourselves. When you have this dangerous mentality it is like a fortress that sets itself up and stops progress, because if progress were made then you wouldn't be a victim. We all play this card to one degree or another unless you have overcome it completely. And that is a beautiful thing. Once you leave that mentality, then you can get down to business. However, as long as you have the "victim card" in your deck, you are subservient to that mentality. That servitude will keep you from where you want to go. Decide right now that you are done with being a victim. You have the power, authority and opportunity to elevate yourself with God's strength towards your destiny. Doesn't God's word say, "If God is for us, who can be against us?" (Romans 8:31). Yes it does. Do you believe it? Grab onto the fact that the Creator of the universe is for you. Although you may have some struggles, you will not be stopped. You are nobody's victim.

After you have chosen change you have to use your strength. Some fool themselves into believing that they don't have the strength. That is not true! You are wonderfully made and have the strength to enact your decision. You are an incredible person who has strength to do so many things of your choosing. If you have given your life to Christ, then Christ's strength is in you. He has the strength. You have what it takes.

To use your strength takes effort. Think of strength like a muscle. The muscles in our bodies are there to move our frame. The bones can't move without our muscles unless someone else moves them. You must summon the effort to move the muscle like you must summon your strength to bring about your will. Your choice is subject to your ability to bring it about, but you are not left without a way to enforce it. Your mind will tell your brain to generate the proper forces necessary to see your choice happen. You have what it takes to spend within your wisely set limits or to perform an act of kindness towards a stranger. You decide, you use your strength, which puts forth the effort to get you want you have chosen. You are not a victim. Your choices determine your future.

There are two types of people who think they don't have the willpower it takes to change. The first type is truly addicted. Whether it is psychologically, physiologically or any other *logically*, they really do have their foot in a trap and they can't get out on their own (more on that later). Is that you? The other type of person has never learned to die to their desires. Maybe it is from a permissive upbringing, or maybe it is because of a super strict, and even abusive upbringing that they rebel against. Whether it has anything to do with their upbringing, they have not learned to deny themselves. Is that you? You buy what you want, you eat what you want, you say what you want to whomever you want; in fact, you are pretty much ruled by what you want. You don't know how to say, "No," to yourself. Let me state this very clearly: you can say, "No," to yourself. You can learn new patterns and live a new life, but it will be painful (and that is what you have wanted to avoid all these years: pain). The only problem is that your selfish desires have caused you more pain than you expected. They have gotten you into bind after bind and now, right now, you have a chance to make the change. You can do it! You can choose to deny yourself. Keep reading and do it—your destiny is waiting for you.

Making a Doable Plan

Once you have concretely decided to move the earth if necessary to make some changes, to get to your next level, to experience more of what we are called to, then you need to make a plan. Reading this book will be beneficial, but you still have to make the changes necessary. It has been said that most self-help books are put down after reading approximately 50 pages. Maybe they are boring, maybe there are no pictures, maybe a lot of things...including people thinking they could change just by reading a few pages and sticking the book under their pillows! If you want something to happen in your life that is going to last, you have to make a plan with determination to carry it out. You know the saying, "If you fail to plan you plan to ... fail."

I suggest a step further than just planning (which is a great step). Make a plan that is doable. If you plan to be a millionaire in six months and you are starting with one dollar, then you had better have a rabbit up your sleeve. If you want to lose 50 pounds in 20 days, then you are going to need surgery. If you want to be married by the end of November when it is October, and you aren't seeing anybody, ahh ... mail order? You get the point. Make your goals reasonable and attainable, and if you can, make them measurable. It should be obvious that people who make plans to carry out what they need to accomplish, in order to have success in many areas of their lives tend to succeed more than those who don't.

For those who are in the trap and seriously can't get out: You need God! The blessing of God's strength cannot be understated. I know that we can make good choices in this life on our own. By saying that, I am not saying that we have our own strength, because I believe that every bit of strength, determination, talent and everything else we have has been given to us by God. However, when we look to Him for strength and for deliverance from a trap in which we find ourselves, we are like super charged humans. God gives His sheep, His children, His mighty working power that is at work within us all the time. That is why Jesus said, "All things are possible to him who believes." (Mark 9:23 NKJV) Everything is possible for us who believe. In other words, nothing is impossible with God. God wants to get us out of any traps that we are in, whether they are addictions to substances or to certain behaviors, whether they are our ways of thinking or ways of relating to others, God wants us to be free! Paul writes, "It is for freedom that Christ has set us free." (Galatians 5:1) Christ came to give us *life* and life to the *full!* We have to get free from any bondage to have everything God has for us, and He knows how to get us free. Trust Him.

Finishing well is a value of mine. I want my marriage to finish well—'til death do us part. I want to finish well financially and leave an inheritance for my children and my children's children. I want to end my days being a kinder and more forgiving man who loves being a part of a community of people. I want to have all my mental capabilities and be physically fit and healthy in the last leg of my journey on this earth. How about you? I most certainly want to meet my Maker, my God, with a smile on my face and joy in my heart because I have attained what I have longed for, to see Him face-to-face. I hope you will reject with me the idea of "over the hill." It's nonsense. (Although the hill does get steeper in many ways.) We are not relegated to a bother of societies; we will be the sages of society. To finish the race well, you have to be well conditioned. Thankfully, God wants you to finish well, so He has equipped you with the propensity to do just that. It is up to you, to me, to all, to make the changes to our lives in order to attain our destiny, our dreams, and God's dreams for us. Whatever changes need to be made, let's make them and live with greatness until we cross the finish line.

2

Torpedoes That Can Sink You

There are things that can sink a big ship. I have watched enough WWII movies and documentaries to see it happen over and over again. Torpedoes aren't small compared to a rowboat, but they are when compared to a huge ship. However they have the power to sink a ship with a properly placed hit. We need not dwell on them, no great admiral ever did, but not to take them into consideration may prove to be dangerous. There are some things that I have already mentioned that can be pitfalls, but here I present a few more that you need to be aware of so you can watch out for them. When you see them coming, either blow them up before they hit you or avoid them.

Happening vs. Atmosphere vs. Culture

If you make your changes a happening then it will last for a short time—maybe. If the happening lasts for a little while it becomes an atmosphere (a new way of thinking). After the new atmosphere has been normalized, it becomes your culture (a new way of living).

One of the problems with diets (a happening) is you go off them eventually. When you go off them you go back to eating the way you did before you figured out you should go on a diet. Then after a while, you go back on the diet…. It is a vicious circle that almost NEVER works. The same is true for everything else in life. Let's say you go to a marriage enrichment weekend. The speakers are great, the education is wonderful and the exercises are just what the doctor ordered. The connection with your spouse looks like it is taking off into new heights—and then you get home. When you get home there are no speakers, no hours carved out for exercises and no emphasis—unless you purposefully make it so. So you do the same things you did before without implementing anything from the weekend into your standard operating procedure. Before long, you are going to need another marriage retreat. Our mindset is so important. Whether it is relational practices, eating plans, spending plans or daily living plans, we can't look at things as temporary. You have to create an atmosphere of how you want to live, which after practiced for long enough, will become a culture.

I will admit that there must be times of special emphasis. These are the times where your determination level is matched by your time and energy commitment in a shorter burst of emphasis. Sometimes you need to do this to push past the roadblocks that come into your life. In our example above, the marriage enrichment can be just that. When you are done with the weekend, however, the status quo has changed; things are different. You were challenged to change the way you conduct your marriage and you (hopefully) implemented those changes. It's like changing the way you are eating. You can either put the stuff you don't want to eat in the garage where it is not so available until you are "done" with your diet, or you can get it out of your house for good and put something else in its place. Say goodbye to your old comfort food, friend.

When I was young, I burned from 4000 to 6000 calories per day. I had a very physical job and then would come home and lift weights with my neighbor. Then I got a little older and started putting on a few pounds and inches. Yet, all I had to do was to cut out chips for a week or two and I would lose 7 lbs. and a half inch or more off my waist. (The real reason for losing the weight was that I didn't want to buy new clothes.) That was in my 30s, but I am in my 50s now. The rules have changed. Those days are gone—forever.

Before having a plethora of kids, maintaining my relationship with my wife was easy. With one or two, it wasn't that hard. We were young and our lives weren't that full. We had game night every Tuesday with Tom and Lynda (which us guys dominated of course). We had plenty of nights at home playing with the kids even though we were very involved in our church. Both of us worked, but something happened and leisure became illusive. We kept having kids. We got more involved in more things. We had less time together and before I knew it, we were partners in life. The romance wasn't gone, but you had to look hard to find it. We lived like many had before us, busy and connecting only after the kids were in bed and my wife was exhausted! Great! Something needed to happen.

Today, if you ask our kids what Monday night is they will instinctively say it's date night for Mom and Dad. We have successfully created a culture in our home of date night. Lora and I also go away about 9 to 10 times per year for an overnighter. Why? Obviously it is to rekindle or keep the fire of romance burning. It is a purposeful and intentional play date with my best friend and lover. We have done it for years. It is culture.

Turning a happening into an atmosphere takes effort. You have to concentrate a bit more than usual because it is easier to slip back into the pattern of old than to create a new one. If you tend to be a negative thinker, to change to a positive thinker is going to take some work. However, if you put the effort into it, thought after thought and day after day, you will have an atmosphere around you of positivity. Strive to let that atmosphere linger and it will become a culture.

I know this guy, Marcus Ellington. He is one of the most positive young men I know. He always has a smile and always has something good to say. I once said something negative while standing next to him. It was one of those complaints that came out as a joke. You know what I mean? Just his presence next to me made me wish I had kept my mouth shut. I believe that is because of his culture of positivity. When you or a group has a culture, everyone around you feels it.

John and Sarah party on the weekends. They hang out with a bunch of friends from college and get together on Friday and Saturday nights to party with them. Sometimes they go to the bar, sometimes to a friend's house. But you know if it is Friday night that John and Sarah are partying and probably trashed. It is their culture. It is their friends' culture. It is what they do and what they are expected to do. When they stay home for the weekend, people are wondering what happened to them. It becomes strange that they didn't "party on" over the weekend.

Culture can be good or bad. It is up to you. Don't be fooled by creating a happening and thinking it will last just because you started it. It usually won't. You can, however, determine what culture you live within. My point in all of this is for you to create a culture of how you want to live. You are the captain of the ship. You determine the course of your life. As the captain you determine what people wear on your bridge (the control center of a ship), how they will address you and what kind of behavior they exhibit. It is all about the culture. It takes choice, effort and strength, but it is so worth it!

A Word About Breaks

If you have created a culture, then breaks are not going to be something on your radar. If you are thinking that you just need a break, a vacation of sorts from life, a break from pursuing your dreams, you may find yourself in no man's land. If break means little or no discipline, it is not a break it is a breakdown. If you are going to relax your life plan so much that it takes no effort, prepare to backslide. Make sure your break isn't a breakdown.

It isn't like you can't miss a date night, or eat something off your eating plan or spend an extra $20 this month. Yet some people tend to "take a break" which means, I am breaking up with you. Remember that? It's the ol' "Dear John" letter without really writing one. It is breaking up with your significant other without having the fortitude to say it.

Sometimes I think we can set such a high standard for ourselves that we nearly burn out. We are trying to make it to the level above our next level in warp speed and we are killing ourselves to get there. Then when we are overwhelmed by it all, we want to take a break from our goals of life. We need to relax and enjoy the journey. It is not meant to be like boot camp all the time. Enjoying a camping vacation instead of a 4 Star resort may be difficult for some, but really, it can be quite enjoyable with the proper attitude.

If you're cutting back on TV and it is Bowl Game season, DVR (so you can skip the commercials) and enjoy more time with your friends and family. If it is the holiday season and you want some sweets and that means a box of See's Candies every week, ask Santa for a new wardrobe, because you are going to need to go up a size. Why not have a treat or two and enjoy? Right now some of you can't believe that I said that people should eat See's Candy during Christmas! I didn't! (If you really need some kind of candy fix, make your own with organic and wholesome ingredients and sweeten it with Stevia). What I am saying is that for some of you, you must have some sort of outlet of the rigor of your life plan when it is under a particularly intense discipline. If that is you, enjoy life, but don't overindulge.

Don't Let a Setback Define You

"Well, I bought some shoes that I shouldn't have, so I might as well buy the dress and the handbag that goes with it." This is not a way to approach your finances let alone life. Yet we tend to give ourselves an excuse with our own failings. Don't do it! You can get back on track no matter what it is. If you spoke negatively and harshly to a co-worker, that doesn't mean that you are so messed up you might as well not try anymore. It is just one or maybe even a couple of failings. What is so bad about that? Really? Why is it that we know we are not perfect but we don't allow ourselves to fall short? That is messed up thinking.

The greatest book of wisdom ever written is the Book of Proverbs. Proverbs 24:16 says that a righteous man falls seven times but rises again. Now that is some truth! Everybody falls, but it is the people who get back up that will be counted among those successful. Allow yourself to be human. Just don't use that as an excuse.

Life Interruptions

Life happens. Things come up that ruin your plans. I was once on a mission trip to Peru and we had a phrase that summed up our daily routine, "cambio de planes"—change of plans. Sometimes things cannot be avoided and those things will put a kink in our plans for our next level in a certain area of life. You are saving great, you are paying off debts, you got a raise and things are looking good, and then it happens: your car engine seizes and it's going to be $2000 to fix it. Your marriage is going great, you are getting all kinds of time with your spouse because of some intentional decisions that you both made and your mother-in-law gets sick and has to move in with you. You have got to stay the course and make some adjustments. It is not always easy, but it can be done. Things are going to happen. You will be cut off at some point on your way to your destination. Find another way! God isn't surprised or caught off guard. Ask Him for a work around. He will give you one.

Expecting Too Much

Expecting overnight change is a pitfall, a torpedo of gigantic proportions. We live in a microwave society where fast food happens at nice sit down restaurants. You can barely finish your salad before your main course comes. We want everything fast and easy. We want to lose 50 pounds in 30 days and keep it off forever. We want to buy it now so we charge it. Our young people want to drive a BMW in high school and get a job paying $80,000 straight out of college. Whatever we want, we want it fast and now and we want it without effort. That is why diet pills like Fen-Phen were so popular. Take a pill, lose weight, and change nothing. So give yourself time, and plenty of it. Setting goals is fine but setting unrealistic timelines will stress you out and could spiral you down into giving up altogether. Change will come. Just take it step by step.

Don't Take on Serious Issues Without Help

Some of you have some very serious issues. You have mental disabilities, emotional trauma and abuse backgrounds, and the list goes on. You may need to engage the services of a professional for certain things. There is no shame in that. I have sat with a counselor to help me a few times in my life when I just couldn't get anywhere by myself. Don't be afraid to ask for help. There are certain things that must be taken seriously enough to solicit some professional help. That is all part of your plan. It is part of the way you are going to get to your next level.

If you have a physical disability, you don't have to stop because you have a disability of some sort. You have to work around it sometimes. You can still have a fitness program if you have bad knees. You can still exercise if you have trouble with your back. In fact, you probably need some therapy on your back (unless your doctor has advised against it) to get to your next level. You have to work with what you have, not throw in the towel because you have problems.

I know a guy who hired a personal trainer and he is wheelchair bound with muscular dystrophy, a debilitating muscular disease. He is doing what he can to stave off this horrific disease. I must say here that if you have something physically wrong with you, a malady, injury or disease of any sort, you need to consult a doctor before you begin any type of exercise program. If your doctor says you can't do anything, but you think you can, get a second opinion.

Focus on one thing at a time. Sometimes having several things that you are trying to change is too much if one of them is a bit overwhelming. Remember that all of the other areas will be positively impacted while you make changes and work on one area. This is especially true if it is a major problem. Any major issue you are having is affecting all of the areas of your life to one degree or another. Engaging in just that area is a good idea if it has been insurmountable your whole life or it will take professional or another type of help to deal with it.

Negative Prophecy Fulfillment

Sometimes our negative attitude can lead to torpedoing ourselves, and then saying to others and to ourselves, that we just can't do it for this reason or for that reason. It is the type of thinking that says that you will try it, however, you don't think you can change. Then you purposefully sabotage yourself to fulfill what you have thought from the beginning.

This kind of thinking can stem from several things including:

- A deep-seated belief that you can't do it

- A deep-seated philosophy that you don't deserve it
- The fear of failing
- The fact that you are plain lazy! Ouch!

Hey, I've been lazy, that is easy to overcome. It is the other deep-seated belief systems that are difficult. If I just called you out, my encouragement is for you to get some help. Either see a counselor, get mentored by an older and wiser friend, or get a book to help you process. Above all else, pray and engage God on the subject. Study the Bible and transform your thinking and belief systems so they line up with God's heart.

All these torpedoes can be shot before it reaches your ship so get your guns out and blow them out of the water!

3

Get Your Freedom

Before we launch into the rest of the book and look at the six areas of life, we have to talk about addictions. This chapter could be a whole book in itself. Maybe this chapter is going to be too simplistic, but my intention is not to give a realistic and vital step-by-step approach or a deep look into addictions. I do, however, understand that many people have addictions and are suffering to one degree or another. The statistics are staggering when you look at them! So I must address this in order to speak to those who need it so they can develop a lifestyle that is *Total Life Pursuit.*

Different Levels of Addiction (A Simple, Non-Therapeutic Definition)

Stage #1: You like it; it gives you pleasure and you continue to choose to do it. Your life continues fine, your friends still like you. You have mutual relationships and not dependent ones. You like to party like a rock star at this level. You love it and think you could say no, but if you do, you are sad, depressed and obsessed about the next opportunity to party or engage in your addictive behavior.

Stage #2: It becomes a part of you. It is your new normal. You can still hold down a job and haven't lost but a few friends who think you are over the top. You have to have it every day or you don't function well. You can probably go a day without it, but why? You may not go through major withdrawals without it, but your life is augmented by doing it or not doing it. It occupies a lot of your thinking throughout the day. Your life is surrounded by it.

Stage #3: You can't live without it. You will cross any line you need to in order to have it or attain it for use. You have lost many things because of it—relationships, housing, jobs, etc... If you don't have it, you go into withdrawals and you cannot function well or at all. In fact, the high you used to get is now your normal unless you push the envelope with either more than normal or longer than normal. It completely rules you. You can't say no to it and you may disguise that by saying you don't want to say no. Your life surrounds it.

There are different types of addictions and there are certainly addictions that harm you more than others. However, whatever they are, they are bad news because they make you their victim. Here is the list of the top addictions in order within the US:

1. Drugs – with prescription drugs leading the way
2. Cigarettes
3. Alcohol
4. Porn
5. Gambling
6. Food – carbs, fast food and junk food
7. Internet/video games
8. TV
9. Shopping
10. Work

We could also throw in looking good and glamorizing ourselves, from plastic surgery to teeth whitening, to hours in the gym, but the above list will suffice.

If you are one who says that you don't have a problem—but deep down you think you might, or other people have told you that you do—then quit for two weeks or one month. If you can't or "you don't want to," then you are hooked! Maybe you are a carbohydrate addict, seriously addicted to carbs—you may indeed need some help. It is very beneficial to deny yourself even on the things that are "just fine" for you to do or ingest. There are even beneficial results of a short food fast (and I am not talking between lunch and dinner), and food is essential for life. If there is something that you depend on too much, try stopping it for a while and see what happens.

I write this short chapter to say that if you are an addict, presently addicted to something and using food, sex, drugs, alcohol, credit or anything else to find pleasure or have redefined normal or worse, then you need to get some help beyond this book. This book and the *Total Life Pursuit* course will help you immensely, but if you are addicted, especially in Stage #3 or even in Stage #2, you need to have someone walk you through to freedom. You are on the road to death! (Even Stage #1 is the road to death). It may not be a physical death, but a death to you, who you are and who you were created to be.

Obviously there is different help for different additions and the level of those additions. Honestly, whether you feel you're addicted or not, I advise everyone to travel through life with others. It is essential for our survival and our thriving to be connected to community. If you are an addict of some sort, join a support group or get some help from a practitioner of some kind. If you are a drug or alcohol addict you need professional help and you know it! I say this to strongly encourage those who need outside help to *go* get it. Asking for help isn't an evil thing, in fact, it is a good thing and takes great courage. The bottom line is that none of us want to be in jail or told what to do. We don't want to be ordered around our whole lives by someone (or in this case—something) that doesn't give a flying rip about us. Whatever you are ruled by, whatever has enslaved you—GO get your freedom!

4

The Whole Person

The beauty of our lives is that we are one. What I mean is that we have many parts, but they are all a part of us. We are so wonderfully made to work in unison with ourselves. Our physical bodies operate at maximum efficiency when they are all working towards the same goal. There is such wonder at all of our different organs working together. It is amazing! Some things we don't even have to think about, like breathing. My brain is working in concert with my nerves and my muscles and my diaphragm and my lungs, which needs my mouth and/or my nose to be open to get air in and get air out. It is amazing. I can hold my breath too. I can override the natural function for a short time, but then my body and brain screams at me to breathe.

There are so many dimensions to life. It is said that we are the sum of all our parts. That is true if you include all the parts. We are made up of both immaterial and material things. Our souls are immaterial and our bodies are very material. All of our parts are so interwoven that they can't be separated. In the same fashion our lives are made up of different areas that interact and correspond to our parts. The six major areas are: spiritual, physical, mental, emotional, financial and relational. Although we can work on them separately, they are a part of us and cannot be disconnected without profound impact.

I have seen something that I believe has become very detrimental to our lives. It is the ability to disassociate. When you are at war or being attacked, you have to be able to separate yourself from the circumstance in order to activate your training to overcome the enemy. When tragedy happens, we have this ability to absorb the hit and continue on. However, we have to deal with it at some point. I believe that God has given us this ability as a coping mechanism for trauma, but we are using it in normal, everyday life. It's like using one of those military grade "bunker buster" bombs to dig a hole to bury your pet. What I believe it has produced are fragmented people who have locked away certain things to never think about them again. Or at least they hope they won't. People have become professionals at burying things that need to be dealt with and the consequences are seen in individuals, families and society.

There is a man who goes to church every Sunday and is "one of the nicest guys." He prays for other people and is an usher at his church. His life away from church is totally stressed out. He is so stressed that it is beginning to take a toll on his marriage. He has some ideas on how to reduce the stress, but he is driven to succeed.

There is a woman, who is a business icon! Everything she touches turns to gold! She has a great attitude and is so positive it is almost annoying. Her marriage, however, is terrible. It is nearly just a facade. All she can think to do is ignore it; although, if she would apply some of the principles of business to her marriage it would begin to grow again.

There is a guy at the gym. He is in such good shape that even the other men admire his physique. He eats well, is disciplined in every area of his physical life, but he is filled with bitterness.

There is a pastor that everyone loves. He is well known, a financial success, and he has a great family who loves each other. He is a little stressed out by the schedule he keeps, but is mostly able to overcome those stressors. The one thing he really struggles with is the fact that he is 50 pounds overweight and horribly out of shape. He knows he shouldn't eat that cake at the church fellowship, but what is the harm with one more piece of cake? After all, everything else is going so well.

Maybe you see yourself in those scenarios, but maybe your scenario is a little different. Whichever is the case, you, like I am, are seeing something. Some people are not just floating down the river of life—the mediocre river. Some people are excelling. They are great at certain things. They have been able to attain a certain level of success in one or two of the six major areas of life. However, they seem to have disconnected some others. Maybe it is because they have no energy left, or maybe it is because they just don't think about it anymore. They have buried it and disconnected. They have cut certain areas of life off from themselves.

If parts are disconnected can they really be a part of the whole? The answer is yes, but they will cause the whole to operate in some sort of dysfunction. You cannot separate your different parts without a death to that which is separated. Think of it like body parts. Every system in your body is created to work together and to feed the eye as well as the toes. You can't get away from the law of connection.

I was talking to a business consultant. He is a workforce engineer. He is in the business of engineering the discontinuity out of businesses so they can operate at maximum efficiency. There is no way for a business to reach its potential if the different departments are not working on the same page. There has to be continuity for things to operate toward maximum destiny.

Let me pound this point again—we are holistic people! Every part of us is connected with the other parts, or at least they are supposed to be. We are not designed to succeed in one or two areas only to ignore the others. We have a problem—we are a disconnected people!

I know people just like those people I talked about above. The examples above are fictitious, but they represent the truth of so many lives. Why should we settle for a less-than-good marriage if we have financial success? Why should the pastor be okay with an unhealthy physical body, or why should any of us settle for being stressed out because we have a job, or a family, or whatever! It is nonsense to think like that as I am sure you will agree, however so many do and I would challenge you to stop reading right now and ask yourself if you have disconnected yourself from excelling in the area of:

- Spiritual life – How is your relationship with God?
- Physical life – How is your fitness and health?
- Mental life – How is your thought life? Is it positive?
- Emotional life – How is your stress level? Do you carry around deadly emotions?
- Relationship life – How is your marriage, your family and your friends?

- Financial life – How are your finances and how is your outlook for the future?

If you aren't thriving in all of them, welcome to the human race! I am not talking about thriving all the time, although it is possible to thrive in all six areas. What I am interested in here in this chapter is, do you give yourself permission to NOT succeed? Have you disconnected one or more of these areas for any reason? Maybe because of your job you can't spend enough time at home so relationships must be compromised or your job stresses you out, but you still have plenty of money. Maybe you have given yourself permission to be out of shape and downright unhealthy because you work so much or study the Bible all the time. It is time to look in the mirror and get honest. Have you given permission to living beneath the bar of great in any area of your life?

It is important to inventory our lives from time to time. In the *TLP: Pursuing Life Workbook*, I ask some very important questions that we should answer bi-annually. Why? So we don't live in deception. The problem with deception is it is deceiving. We don't know we are being deceived because we are deceived. That is one of the problems that come with disconnecting, compartmentalizing and burying things. We begin to tell ourselves that we are okay long enough that we begin to believe what we say. We convince ourselves that this is the best it can be. We acquiesce to a lower standard of living and call it normal.

It is the same mentality that happens in some women who are abused. I have some friends who are cops and they will tell you that domestic calls are dangerous. Sometimes when they arrest the abusive boyfriend or husband (yes, it could be the woman who is an abuser as well), the girlfriend or wife will attack them. Most of us say, "Huh? What gives? That guy deserves to go to jail and she should be happy about it." Maybe she fears his release or maybe she has believed the lie that she has told herself (not all victims, just some believe this), "He tells me he loves me, but sometimes he just loses his cool." What she has done is to define "bad" as normal. Sad.

Some in the church are starting to get nervous because of this holistic approach to life. The church has thrown out some good doctrine in order to stay away from eastern religion. We have thrown out good herbal remedies with some other practices because it's associated with a culture that practices a different religion. Eastern religions say that human beings are holistic. Is that a reason to abandon this way of thinking? Christians cannot be afraid of this thinking because its roots are found in the Bible!

In 1 Thessalonians 5:23 it says, "May your whole spirit, soul and body be kept blameless…" I cannot be more emphatic here; we are holistic people! Every part of us is connected with the other parts, or at least they are supposed to be. We are not designed to succeed in one or two areas, only to ignore the others. Neither are we designed to ignore any area of our lives even though it "won't be with us in heaven." It is here now!

The Six Areas Defined

Spiritual

In my thinking there is nothing more important than your relationship with the God of the Universe. He created you like Him, in His likeness, so you could have relationship with Him and He with you. This area properly defined is about your connection to God.

If you have a different belief system, as Yahweh would, I give you full latitude to believe what you want. If you don't agree with my theology of God in totality or you are just not there yet, keep reading!

Physical

Admittedly, I am most fascinated with this area. The more I learn about our bodies, the more amazed I am. We are the most delicate, organized, complex piece of matter in the solar system. We will be talking about health as it relates to our entire physical function. From sickness and immune function, to fitness, strength and stabilization, what we eat, and how we live our lives in order to maintain and gain in the area of our physical health.

Mental

How you think, you will be. That is an undeniable fact that is in the book of Proverbs. In fact it says that as you think in your heart, you are (Proverbs 23:7). We will see just how true that is, but suffice to say that our thinking and our brain activity are included in this section. You control how you behave, how you move, how you speak and how you live. We will be diving into some science and theories that are incredible and which bring hope to all of us.

There are two different thoughts in science and psychology. Mind controls matter, or matter controls mind. In other words, either our soul (mind) controls our brain or our brain (matter) controls our soul. I believe that our soul, our thinking and volitional center, controls our brain. Therefore the mind and the will give birth to your brain activity. You can control more than you think!

Emotional

Although emotions are chemical signals attached to thoughts, most people consider them to be almost intangible. They are not. There are many emotions that will negatively affect our lives including bitterness, hatred and others. Yet I have determined to focus on stress even though stress is a bodily function based on your thinking. Stress causes such havoc in our lives and it is in my mind, which is born out in various studies, the greatest contributing factor today to so many ills, physically, relationally, mentally, financially and even spiritually. It may not be a pure emotion, and as you will see, it is actually physical, but I have included it here in the emotional section because it is widely thought as an emotional response and guides so many of our negative emotions.

Relational

The importance of relationships cannot be overstated. We are designed for relationship. It is a common belief that without community of some sort after retirement, you will decline rapidly. Friendships and family are essential for our lives to thrive. For our purposes we will focus on three main relationships:

- Marital
- Parent/child
- Friendships

Financial

Some of you are asking, "What do finances have to do with my being?" For centuries it may not have had the importance and emphasis that it does now. We live in the west where finances are a big deal. Whether it is buying a house or car, or it is begging for your next meal, finances have become part of us in a large way. We spend a minimum of 25%, and usually closer to 33%, of our adult lives getting ready for, and driving to and from work. For the high achievers it is even more. What we do with our money can create freedom or enslavement. Important area? Absolutely!

I am sure you are beginning to see the interconnectedness. Let's begin to connect some dots. Our spiritual life can affect every area. If we believe that God created us to love, we will be more apt to love. If we believe that God is for us and wants the best for us, we will have more of a positive outlook. If we are convinced that God wants us to be amply supplied for, we won't overwork, or stress out about money. If we are thinking positively, then we will be less stressed and more pleasant to be around. If we are physically healthy we will save on finances and be able to enjoy life, which will allow us more pleasure, which will keep our neurotransmitters balanced in our brain, which will give us all kinds of benefits. I could go on, but you get the point.

Oh, let's go on for just a minute more. If you are thinking negatively, then you are projecting negativity to others. That negative thinking has a lot to do with your health. Thinking also controls your stress levels. It also bleeds into all the other areas. You get a flat tire and you get out and you are mad. You kick the tire and break your toe. Now you have to go to the doctor and pay him. Of course your stress level is high because you were going on an anniversary trip and going to hike the Grand Canyon. Now your marriage is stressed! All because of... not a flat tire, but an uncontrolled thought.

It is not okay to settle for mediocre in any area precisely because you cannot contain the mediocre into that area. It will bleed into the other areas of life sooner or later. There is a snowball effect in our souls when we disconnect one or more areas. It just keeps getting bigger and bigger. If your marriage is on the rocks, then sooner or later other relationships will be affected—at least your in-laws! If you get a divorce your financial outlook just took a major hit, as did... well, you know where I am going.

The human personality is broken. I think we just come out that way. Psychologists and philosophers may debate this assertion, but we can all agree that people have brokenness by the time they hit their adult years to one extent or the other for some reason. I believe that the way we compartmentalize the different areas of life produces a discontinuity within the individual that fractures him or her all the more. Before long people settle for mediocre or even below mediocre in these broken parts of their life. They have another area or areas that they are doing all right or even good in, and that becomes good enough for them. For example, a father may think: "My kids don't like me, but at least I'm rich." That is some messed up thinking. How do you think so many fathers can abandon their children? They bury their instinct, their God-given desire to father their children, and disconnect it from the rest of their lives. There is this mentality that says abundance, or flourishing, isn't important in all areas of my life. It recites that "things happen" way of thinking and that there is nothing you can do. Sad.

A Word to My Christian Brothers and Sisters

How is it that we (as Christians) are no different than the world in many facets of life? Some have mastered the art of compartmentalization and we know how to look good and sound good around church folk. Do you know that you are 50% more likely to be obese if you regularly attend church? How can that be? I understand how it happens, but I don't understand how we could think it is okay. Our divorce rate is the same as our societies'. Something has got to happen. We have to find our way to God again and listen to His heart for us. He wants to prosper us and give us hope. We are the hope bringers!

Jesus is our Savior and our Lord. Lord means decision maker. That means God gets to organize our day. He gets to choose what we think about and dwell on. He gets to choose our food and fitness regimen. He gets to direct us into a great marriage and into lasting friendships. And finally, He gets to tell us what to do with our money! How have we gotten so off track? We have assumed control of our own lives in a take-over fashion. Yes we are the captains of our own ships, but we are to take directions from Papa God on how to steer. Surrender is a word that comes to mind here. I don't say this tritely. It is difficult to be in a state of surrender, but ultimately that is exactly what brings us to an elevated life. When we give it away, it is returned to us 30, 60, 100 fold. It's a good deal; let's take it—again.

The Need for Chapters

After all this talk about the importance of being connected, I am about to separate each of the six areas into separate chapters. It is what authors do! There are some fantastic reasons for doing so with which I am sure you will agree.

1. Assessing each area separately is the only way to attain a good understanding of where you are at in that area and where you want to be. Basically, you can only think about one thing at a time, at least in a deep and meaningful way, which is what we want to happen.

2. Although you can work on two things in the same day or even at the same time (like walking and chewing gum— you can do that, right?), it is helpful to cast vision for yourself and set goals in each of the six areas separately. The really cool thing is that they are all connected so when you work on your body, your mind and emotions will benefit, or when you work on reducing your stress level, you marriage and body will benefit. So the effects of the improvements in one area will show up in other areas as well!

3. Writing a book with no chapters would just be plain weird. Imagine reading a book and wanting to read just one more chapter before bed, except that there are no chapters! You would be up all night!

5

Spiritual Part of the Whole

As you have already discerned, I have a Christian belief system. I don't apologize for it. If you don't have that particular belief, you might be tempted to skip this chapter all together. I think that the spiritual life of a person is the most important area and will strongly affect the other areas, or at least it should. I encourage you to make this your starting point. There will be good practices within this chapter that you will be able to use. So read on.

When it comes to this area—the spiritual portion of life—you, like me, have to get to our next level no matter what level you are on right now. There are many different belief systems that people wholeheartedly accept. There are atheists, not acknowledging the existence of God. There are agnostics, who don't know and don't express an opinion on whether there is a God or not, and there are others who have a belief system based on eastern religious thought. There are dozens of major theological views and hundreds of different ways of practicing them including Judaism and Christianity.

The only place you can start in any area is where you are at right now. Unlike a race where you have to go to an appointed starting point, in life you start from where you are currently. This is no different for any of the six parts and only makes sense, right? The great thing is that God accepts you for who you are and where you are in life. There is no expectation that if you aren't (fill in the blank) that you can't go anywhere from there! So wherever you are, let's begin there.

The way I view things, and I believe the way God views things, is that the most important principle in the area of your spiritual life is your connection with God. You can do good acts all day long and you can be a kind and gentle person. You can give money to the poor, but without a genuine and tangible relationship with the Living God, you are missing out. There are things that I will recommend become a part of your life, but if you divorce those things from being connected to God, then it isn't all for nothing, but you have missed the most important thing: relationship with God, with Papa.

Relationship for many has been replaced by do's and don'ts, a way to live and conduct your life. Jesus came to connect us to and show us the heart of the Father, but some interpret that to mean He (Jesus) came to show us how to live right. Wrong! He came to bring us back to the relationship that we lost many millennia ago. Honestly, do we think God created this earth with all of its beauty and grandeur, then created us and placed us here and said, "Take care of it, I'll see you when you die?" I don't think so. We are created in His image so that we can relate to one another. I know that He is God and perfect and all that comes with that, and I am not, but there are qualities about us humans that are God-like. His image is in us. He perceives things, so he gave us our senses. He laughs, so He gave us emotions. He loves, so He gave us the capacity and propensity to love. He loves beauty and so do we! So the question that is begging is: what happened? This topic could be a book in itself. What we will focus on is how do we get close to God again. How can I have a close relationship with God? How can I exchange the God that is far away somewhere (the big man upstairs), and is "too good for me unless I am doing good things" way of thinking, for a loving relationship?

Everything flows from relationship with God. Over and over in the New Testament it tells us that if we are *in* Christ we have everything. It is a relationship and a union of ourselves to Jesus Christ that counts. The question that will be answered is how do we attain our maximum relationship or maximum closeness with God. Below is my prayer for all of us.

¹⁴For this reason I kneel before the Father ¹⁵from whom his whole family in heaven and on earth derives its name. ¹⁶I pray that out of his glorious riches he may strengthen you with power through his Spirit in your inner being, ¹⁷so that Christ may dwell in your hearts through faith. And I pray that you, being rooted and established in love, ¹⁸may have power, together with all the Lord's holy people, to grasp how wide and long and high and deep is the love of Christ, ¹⁹and to know this love that surpasses knowledge—that you may be filled to the measure of all the fullness of God. (Ephesians 3:14-19)

This relationship with God has a starting point: Jesus the Messiah. It is through his life and sacrifice for us that we come into restored relationship with our Maker. In verse 17 above the word for dwell is *katokesai*. It means to settle down and be at home. Now read it again. Jesus wants to settle down and be at home in your hearts. That is why we use the phrase "give our hearts to Jesus." Our hearts are the center of our being, our core, who we really are. That is where Jesus wants to be at home. Do you see it? He wants to be with the real us.

When I am at home I walk over to the fridge and get out what I want and consume it. I don't ask anybody. There are certain people who feel so at home in my house they do the same thing. Have you ever felt that free at someone else's house? That is the way Jesus wants to feel at your home, at your core. When we use phrases like "the big guy upstairs" we keep God at arm's length. I am afraid some have consumed the Kool-Aid, because that is not love and that is not close. Imagine a marriage like that. Maybe you have experienced one or know of one like that. Not good, huh? Exactly. That is not how God intended it to be, with Him or in a marriage.

In verse 18 above we are supposed to grasp something. What are we supposed to grasp? Go back and look. I am not giving you the answer. To grasp is to lay hold of, to seize, to take possession of, to apprehend. Have you ever watched Dog the Bounty Hunter? He hunts down and apprehends people. When he apprehends them, they are in his custody. He chases, searches, and he strategizes to get the fugitive. That is the picture of apprehending the love of Christ. Once you get it, it is yours.

God's love is not conditional. It does not come with a set of

43

expected behaviors in order to keep it. In fact God's Word says:

> [35]*Who shall separate us from the love of Christ? Shall trouble or hardship or persecution or famine or nakedness or danger or sword? ...* [38]*For I am convinced that neither death nor life, neither angels nor demons, neither the present nor the future, nor any powers,* [39]*neither height nor depth, nor anything else in all creation, will be able to separate us from the love of God that is in Christ Jesus our Lord.* (Romans 8:35, 8:38-39)

Closeness with God is shown all throughout the Bible. From Genesis where God talked face-to-face with Adam and Eve, to Revelation when we will see Him face-to-face again, God wants to be with His people. God is and has been looking for people who would have relationship with Him—from Abraham who God decided to birth a nation through, to Peter who became the chief apostle in Jerusalem. What was so special about Abraham? Why did God choose Him? We may not know every reason, but we do know a couple, the first one being that Abraham responded to God. He trusted Him and went where God instructed him. He was far from perfect, but he is the father of faith. Peter was a loose cannon and denied Jesus in His most vital hour. He wasn't perfect either, but he responded when Jesus said "Follow me," and again when Jesus restored him after the denial (John 21:19). When the children of Israel were in the desert after being delivered from Egypt, God wanted to be right there. He instructed Moses to build him a tent so His people would have the visual evidence that God wanted to be close to them. Jesus, the God-man came to dwell among men. I could go on and on. God wants to be close to you.

The ideal relationship with God would be Adam's before his rebellion. He:

- Was blessed
- Was free
- Had no impulsion to sin
- Had dominion
- Was fruitful
- Had a perfect wife! He was the perfect husband.
- Had everything made to his liking

- Had everything and it was perfect
- Had everything he needed
- Actually walked and talked with God
- Had close friendship with God

Sin entered in and messed up everything. Do you think that God doesn't like sin because of some kind of holiness complex of His? He hates sin because it messes up the people He loves—us. So many of the above things were lost. Jesus came and restored everything but not in the same way—yet.

We don't have a perfect world, but:

- We are blessed – we have to believe for it
- We are free – we have to walk in it
- We have the ability to choose NOT to sin
- We have dominion – but we have to take it
- We are fruitful – we have to exercise it
- We have all that we need – we have to believe for it and work for it
- We can walk with God closely – hear his voice (inside of us) and experience His presence
- We can be close with Him

I have talked a lot about closeness. What does that mean to you? When you have a close friend, what does that mean? When you are close with your brother or your mother, what does that connote? Sometimes when we think about God and closeness for some reason we redefine the word. There is something inside of us, if we will allow it to, that cries out for God's presence. Haven't you ever wanted to see Him, hear Him or feel Him? Moses said, I don't want to go if you don't go with me. (Exodus 33:15) That is the cry of our heart if we will allow it to be. If we can get rid of the wrong beliefs, release our shame and be fully devoted to Him, we will want His presence. James writes, "Draw near to God and He will draw near to you." (James 4:8 NKJV)

Have we settled for knowledge of God instead of His presence? If we have, we have lost so much. Don't get me wrong, it is good to believe in God and it is good to trust your eternal future to God, but is that it? Really? Now I should just study and learn about God? As

Moses said in that same passage in Exodus 33:16, "What else will distinguish me and your people from all the other people on the face of the earth [if your presence isn't with us]?"

We find joy in His presence (Acts 2:28, Psalm 16:11). In fact we are filled with it. Nehemiah tells us that the joy of the Lord (which we get in His presence) is our strength. There is no end to the benefits of staying close to God. We are renewed in hope, in strength, in love, in peace and a couple hundred other things. So how do we get there and stay there?

Well, first you get a good Bible reading plan and…NOT! I am not saying you shouldn't read the Bible, of course you would. It is history. It is wisdom. It is God's love letter to you. It tells you who He is and what He is really like. It tells you who you are so you can stop believing that you are the same old person who always blows it when…. Undoubtedly you will read it. You would be foolish not to. It is all in how you read it. But there is something that must come first.

> [19]*Therefore, brothers and sisters, since we have confidence to enter the Most Holy Place by the blood of Jesus,* [20]*by a new and living way opened for us through the curtain, that is, his body,* [21]*and since we have a great priest over the house of God,* [22]*let us draw near to God with a sincere heart and with the full assurance that faith brings, having our hearts sprinkled to cleanse us from a guilty conscience and having our bodies washed with pure water.* [23]*Let us hold unswervingly to the hope we profess, for he who promised is faithful.* (Hebrews 10:19–23)

If we are unsure of how we can justly get close to God, we will continue to keep Him at arms distance. We will want Him to stay in another planetary system on His throne. If you can get this, you will be free from trying to *do* all the right things. I know that people are probably cringing every time I say something like that. They are afraid that people won't act right or do right if we don't tell them to. There is an old saying that goes like this: no matter how much you bark you won't become a dog, but if you are a dog, you naturally bark. If we can understand and apprehend the fact that Jesus did all the work, then we won't get trapped in the *I-have-to-be-good-to-get-close-to-God* thinking, and we won't have the opinion that we can do whatever the heck we want to, and live close to God.

The picture here is that we have been washed and we are to hold unswervingly to this hope, which is a fact. We are cleansed from a guilty conscious. Why invite it back? When we get the revelation that we are accepted because of what Jesus did, then we are set free to be who we are made to be! We will naturally live out the life that God put in us and we won't be afraid when we stumble or when we purposefully do something foolish, sinful, death causing, immoral or anything else, to come right back to Papa. Not in some kind of cheap grace way, but in a, "Dang, I wish I wouldn't have done that, that was dumb. Help me, Papa. I don't want to live like that." The trick is to come back and not to stay away. When we don't get this revelation, that it is Christ that has done the work, we don't want to face God with our sin and our failings. We stay away, distant, and it *gets worse*.

It is time to come back. It is time for us to stop looking at our own lives and look to God our Father who sent His Son so we could be close with Him. It is time to forget the past and move forward, to embrace God because that is what He wants. He wants your embrace. John writes in Revelation that God stands at the door and is knocking. He wants you to let Him in. He wants to eat with you and hang out (Revelation 3:20). What a great picture? This is the starting point—Jesus, our sacrifice for sin. He has made us clean forever. He has washed us and given us His Spirit. He has given us a new heart. He has made us free to hang out with God with confidence. Let's do it!

Although I must say that being close with God sometimes messes things up. It is hard to be a jerk when God is with you. Honestly, I think that is one of the biggest reasons why people keep God at arm's length. They want to do what they want to do without any interruption. It is not worth it. We were made to be close to God. Our bodies and our minds were made to follow God's wisdom. We were made to be close to God and accept what that closeness necessitates—obedience. Before you say, "There he goes with the thou shalts," you need to see things from God's perspective. If your kids wanted to go in the middle of a four-lane busy street and play around with the oncoming traffic, you would say that obedience to the no-playing-in-the-street rule would be pretty important. Every bit of God's wisdom that He gives us is for our own good. He is just trying to keep us out of the street so we don't get killed.

So how do you do it? What are the practical steps after you accept the above as truth? How can I get my relationship with God on the next level? What do you do? It is only after you are convinced that you can't do anything to be "good enough" that you can move to the next step. You have to learn who you are. When you become convinced that you are a different person, a new creation, with a new heart and new proclivities, then you will start to act like it. It is like a person who was given a great inheritance, millions of dollars, yet they still dress in old cloths that are worn and they live in a rented run down house. They eat like they are poor and they act like they are poor, turning down invitations by friends to go have some fun for the day because it would cost money. I am not saying that you should spend all of your money, but for goodness sakes, you should live like you are and not how you used to be. If you had $5 million in the bank would you turn down a night out of bowling because it costs too much? Once we become convinced that we are the new guy (or gal) and not the old one, we will start to expect ourselves to act like them. Is this making sense?

Accelerating your relationship with God to the next level, and then the next level, will become natural. You are at home with God and He is at home with you, in your life. You have made peace with Him so now you can talk with Him all the time. You begin to believe for the good things that He has always wanted to give you, but none is as good as feeling close with Him.

How would you accelerate your relationship with a person? How about a perspective spouse? I remember what I did. I saw Lora (my wife) every chance I got. I talked to her nearly daily. I worked the graveyard shift and she worked the day shift, so I went to sleep as soon as I got home so I could be awake while she wasn't working. I made time for her. I ate with her, I took her bowling, or to the movies, or down to the beach and we walked together. Why would it be any different with God? The concepts are the same. The funny thing is that when I first started dating Lora I wasn't totally myself around her. There is a little bit of impressing going on. With me, you pretty much get what you see. I am not much for pretension. However, I thought she could be the one and I had to catch her. Silly, huh? After I was secure in her love for me, I began to relax and let my hair down. That didn't mean I was mean or thoughtless, but I was myself—warts and all.

Again, it's the same thing with God. Just be who you are. You don't have to talk or pray in some other kind of language with *shalts* and *doest*. Are those even words? Be yourself! It is not like he doesn't know the real you. You are not going to fool Him. So act natural, but with some reverence. He is not your basketball playin' buddy, he is more like your coach. The closeness is there, however there is a respect that will be shown because, after all, He is God. Not way up there, but right here beside you.

I know many great men of God. Ralph Moore is one of them. I'll never forget what he told a small group of guys about Bible reading. He said, "Read until you are blessed." That was a concept I have never heard of. I thought you were supposed to read a chapter a day or something like that. Read until you are blessed. Wow! I am not saying that Bible reading schedules are bad. I have used them to discipline myself to read the Bible in a year. It was a great tool. Some people (like me) need a schedule to help them shoot for something. However, having said that, reading until you are blessed is something that can free the performance personality. Just today I was reading and I got stuck. I won't go into the revelation I had never seen before despite reading the book of John probably a hundred times, but I stopped. I thought about it. I journaled. I blogged. I thought about it from different angles. I was listening for a lesson, like a teacher pointing out something significant to understand. My encouragement to you is: read until you are blessed. When something pops out at you, you can stop or you can go on, but be sure to come back to it when you are done reading. That has happened to me in the first three verses and I almost feel guilty not reading more. I denied that feeling and just let what I had learned soak in me. I thought about it, going over and over it in my mind. Enjoying the lesson. I like to journal, to write about what God is teaching me. So I write. When appropriate, I share what I have learned.

Read to experience His Word in your life. See the heart of God in what you are reading. Seek the understanding of what makes God tick. Especially how he feels and how he thinks about you. I have had the pleasure of hanging around Jack Hayford for several weeks. He is a giant in the faith and it was such a privilege to have him talk to a small group of leaders for hours on end. Although I am interested in what he has to say about certain things because I highly value his opinion, what I really wanted was to understand how this great man processed his thoughts. How did he think about things? How did he approach different issues of life? There wasn't enough time for him to tell us all that he believed about everything. But if I could watch the wheels turning in his head, heart and spirit, then maybe I could gain the impartation that I was seeking. It is similar with God. Although I want to know what God thinks about everything so I can make sure I think like Him, I want to know the person behind the thinking. I want to know what makes God tick. I want to know his heart. Then I will be able to know what He would think about something even if I have never read about it specifically.

To summarize, read the Word of God, it is in the Bible. Read it until you are blessed. When something pops out or interests you or you think God is trying to show or tell you something, stop reading and start engaging. Think about it and talk with God about it. Finally, I encourage you to journal as well. If you are not into that, then don't do it unless God tells you to. If you hate writing with a pen and paper, use your iPad, computer or smart phone.

That brings us to talking with God. Prayer. There are so many things to say here but let's keep it simple. If you are going to get close with God then you not only have to pray (which is talking), but you have to listen. Do you hear God audibly? I have never. Some have, but it is rare. So, how do you hear him? It is that voice on the inside of you. It is the impression that you sense, the thoughts that come. How do you know it is God? Practice.

There are three main voices you hear on the inside of you. It is either God, the devil (more accurately his representative), or it is you. You will begin to see the difference between evil and God pretty quickly. As you grow and as you learn of God, you will know what His character would or wouldn't say. The tougher thing to discern is, is that God or is that me. That is tough and only comes through time and relationship. The one thing that I can tell you is that the more pure your motives are, the clearer it is who is talking. When you desperately want to hear God and do exactly what He wants, it is easier to hear Him. When you are involved, when you really want a certain something, it gets more difficult.

Not long ago I was away with my wife and my good friend Kevin let me use his BMW. That thing is a rocket ship—fast and fun. I am older now and I am not a big speeder—much. I was traveling home on highway 1 in CA. I was following a car going 3-5 mph under the speed limit. (Imagine that.) So after some miles I got an opportunity to pass. I pushed that accelerator to the floorboard and was jerked back in my seat a bit as the car downshifted and began to fly. I don't know how fast I was going, but I got around him pretty quick. After I had passed him a thought came into my head. Slow down quickly, use your brake. Within milliseconds I thought I had observed two police vehicles in the last two miles and it would be safe to coast down to 55 instead of braking. Something told me… You know what happened next, I saw the CHP coming the other way. It was too late to brake. I got a ticket. (The first one in 15 years.) What killed me more than anything thing was, *Something* told me I should have applied my brake to slow down. Something. I am convinced that *Something* is another name for God. *Something* told me not to date that girl; *Something* told me not to buy that car from that guy; *Something* told me I should have ducked…

Another thing I do is to act on it like it is God. I'll know soon enough if it is. If it isn't, oh well, it was an honest mistake. It's not like God is going to leave you hanging. He doesn't say, "Well you really blew it this time. You thought it was me, but it wasn't. I know you were just trying to obey me, but, well, you are on your own. That will teach you." God isn't like that. When you move forward based on what God is saying, you will learn what was Him and what was you. You will hear it. You will know it. You will know it is God.

Try not to make your prayer time about your needs. You can include them, but when that is all you talk to God about, what kind of relationship is that? That is not one you want to have with anybody else. Talk with Him like you would a friend. Laugh with Him and crack jokes or point out funny things to Him. When walking through the zoo ask Him what He was thinking when He created the anteater or the sloth. Draw Him into your life experiences. Thank Him—for everything—all the time. When something is really cool, like a sunset or sunrise, tell Him about it. Then tell Him you love Him. I know this is different for some of you, but don't shrink back, get to the next level!

Worship is a word that has great meaning. It means to come toward, to bow down, to kiss, to adore. When people hear the word worship in a church, they think singing. There is nothing wrong with that because hopefully singing hymns or modern worship songs brings you closer to God. If they do, they are doing what they were meant to do. Personally, music speaks to me. I love worship music. I play guitar and love playing and singing to God. I love putting on worship music and singing along in worship (coming close to God, adoring Him). It is the way I connect. Maybe you are like me and worship is the most conclusive way to connect with God, to come close to Him. You get lost in the song and then just begin to speak to Him, pouring your heart out to Him. Sometimes you are so touched in your heart and/or your spirit or wherever, that you are raptured to a place that it is just you and God. The whole world disappears from your mind. I love those times!

There has got to be a place where you can really let it go. Sing your heart out. Play the music loud. Get there. If you are not into that kind of thing, do it anyways. He is worthy of it. It is impossible to get to the next level or have any change at all if you keep doing what you have been doing and it hasn't produced any fruit. So you may have to change things up a bit.

What follows are not formulas; they are ideas, suggestions, strategies to help you get closer. If they are used as formulas, then you may be falling into the trap of doing all the right things while your heart is not there. Jesus had something to say about that—saying all the right things but having your heart be far from Him. Remember, this is heart-to-heart stuff.

Reading the Bible

Read the Bible until you are blessed. Start with Proverbs and John. You can read the corresponding day-to-chapter in Proverbs because there are 31 chapters. Read through John a couple of times and then move on to Mark. Do the same with Matthew and Luke until you have lived in the gospels for a while. Maybe four to six months. Get rid of all of your preconceived notions, your understandings that really aren't yours, they are someone else's. Come to the Word of God and ask Him to speak to you. Get to know Jesus. He said, if you have seen me, you have seen the Father (John 14:7).

There are several journaling methods to help people who have a hard time knowing what to write. If that is you, try this one. If it works for you, then keep doing it. If it doesn't, try something else.

S – See what God is speaking to you. In other words, what stands out as you read? Pick one scripture that moved you or stood out to you and write it down.

O – Observe the context. What is going on in the passage or the verse? Write down your observations.

A – Apply it to your life. Write out how this verse can be applied to your life, or better yet how it will be applied to your life.

P – Pray. Write a short prayer to God in reference to what you just learned, apprehended and were blessed by God's Word. Thank Him for giving you understanding of his Word.

Praying

Talk with God. If you need a format for a while, start with what is called the Our Father prayer or the Lord's Prayer as a model. Don't just memorize and repeat it, but use it as a template to pray by. It will look something like this:

- Start with praise, worship and adoration. Talk with God here about His goodness.
- Surrender and ask for God to invade your life and others. Talk with God about life. Relate things to Him and listen to what He says. You can name your friends and family and even cities and ask for God to do certain things in their lives.
- Ask for your daily needs, and the needs that are coming up. Not just material, but all of your needs.
- Thank God for everything that relationship with Him brings including forgiveness.
- Ask Him to cleanse you from the actions in your life that

bring, or have brought, yuckiness.

- Forgive everybody. Do it by name if you are holding something against anybody else.
- Ask God to guide you and strengthen you, and to bring Himself glory through your life.

Don't let that model create an impersonal environment for prayer. Prayer is talking. Talking with a close friend. This is just a suggestion (a good one since Jesus gave it), to keep your prayers from being 30 seconds and a list of needs and desires.

You can also pray the Word of God. Take the Bible and open to a passage of scripture and pray it. For example, look up Psalm 128. Your prayer would go something like this (only longer): "God, pour out your blessing on me for I do fear (reverence, awe) you. I do walk in your ways! I am blessed. Thank you that my labor will pay off. Promote me, oh God, in your time. Show me how to create more wealth. May that wealth go well with me and not trap me into trusting it. Thank you for my wife and that she is so fruitful. Increase her fruit! May everything she does produce great dividends."

I think you get the picture. Thank Him, pray for wisdom to cooperate with His blessing and ask for it in great measure.

In all of this remember that closeness with God is key. It is the quintessential reason that we were created. Another way to put it is, we were created for relationship with our God, our Maker, our Papa. Don't lose that. It is the essential truth of life.

There may be some of you that haven't made the decision to give your life to Christ. You are either not convinced or have another belief system all together. My encouragement to you is to read the book of Proverbs. Read it every day and glean from it. It is and has been an accepted book of wisdom and sage advice for thousands of years. Enjoy the practical advice that is really more spiritual than one might think.

6

Physical Part of the Whole

There is good news for you today. You determine how you live your life! Okay, maybe I have said that before, but it is worth saying again. Your physical body is so adaptive, so reactive, so wonderfully made, that the possibilities for great health and fitness are mind blowing. The promise of health is not some pie-in-the-sky concept, it is palpable; it is within your reach. It is there for the taking and those who choose to go after it will get it. The more you go after it, the healthier you become.

God Loves Your Body

Before we launch into the amazing and exciting world of health, I need to address a group of people—Christians. So many Christians think that the body means little to God, and therefore to them, because of their theological viewpoint. So here is a quick theological check up for those who struggle with emphasizing the body as something that needs our thoughtful and disciplined care.

> God saw all that he had made, and it was very good. And there was evening, and there was morning—the sixth day. (Genesis 1:31)

God thought our bodies were pretty awesome. He still does. They are at least as good as the Grand Canyon, or the Swiss Alps, or the Ursa Major Constellation (home to the Big Dipper), and I would argue that it is even more amazing than all of these. God created our bodies; therefore, He loves our bodies.

For I am the Lord who heals you. (Exodus 15:26 NKJV)

In the Hebrew language, "the Lord" in this instance is a compound name, which God gave to himself: God-healer. That is who He is. His name, according to what He said, means *bringing healing and health.* Let that register for a moment. Yahweh calls Himself Healer.

>*[7]Do not be wise in your own eyes; fear the Lord and shun evil. 8This will bring health to your body and nourishment to your bones.* (Proverbs 3:7–8)

>*[20]My son, pay attention to what I say; turn your ear to my words. [21]Do not let them out of your sight, keep them within your heart; [22]for they are life to those who find them and health to one's whole body.* (Proverbs 4:20–22)

The emphasis is the health of your body. God again tells us that He cares deeply about your bodily health by telling you how to attain it. In these two scriptures health comes from fearing the Lord (being convinced that God means what He says), paying attention, listening closely, and keeping His words within your heart.

>*[19]Or do you not know that your body is a temple of the Holy Spirit within you, whom you have from God? You are not your own, [20]for you were bought with a price. So glorify God in your body.* (1 Corinthians 6:19–20 ESV)

Jesus precious blood shed on the cross bought all of you, including your body. Here it simply says that your body is not your own and deserves honor (value) because of the value that God places on it. It also tells us to bring glory to God in our body.

>*I beseech you therefore, brethren, by the mercies of God, that you present your bodies a living sacrifice, holy, acceptable to*

God, which is your reasonable service. (Romans 12:1 NKJV)

What is supposed to be presented as a living sacrifice? Our bodies. God cares about your body. I could go on and on with verses throughout the Bible, but I will save that for another book. God loves your body and cares for your body, and the health of your body is on the concern list for God. He wants you to be healthy and vital!

As you can see, God cares about our bodies and our health, just like we do. He put the impulse within us to maintain health. We may say that we don't care, but we care deeply when things go wrong with our body. It is like breathing. We think little about it until we can't breathe. I have been in some pretty rough surf before. I can tell you, when you are getting tumbled by the ocean and you have no idea which way is up or when you are going to get your next breath, you panic. Everything within you wants to reach the surface and take a breath. What seems like an eternity is really only 10 seconds but we have this mechanism inside of us that wants to be able to breathe. Big wave surfers practice being underwater holding their breath for minutes. They practice not panicking. We must admit our great desire for physical health and fitness and practice it, so when the big wave holds us under for two minutes, we know we have trained for that and can handle it. Within every person is the desire to be healthy, fit and vibrant.

Proprioception

I came across this word in my studies to become a personal trainer. What I have come to realize is that proprioception is not only an exercise physiology word, but it is an important concept in all of life. Properly defined it means: "The cumulative sensory input to the central nervous system from all mechanoreceptors that sense body position and limb movement"[1]. This is important to athletes and personal trainers, and anybody who wants to get in total shape as opposed to just build muscles or lose weight. It strikes me that without proprioception the body cannot work properly because it doesn't know where it is and what it is doing. In fitness it is your neuromuscular evaluation. I propose that we gain a little perception of where we are with a true evaluation of our health. Just like within our bodies we have to constantly evaluate our body position and limb movement, in life we have to honestly evaluate our state of health.

Are you healthy? Are you overweight? Are you out of shape? Somehow when we come to an occasion that we do answer these questions, we either excuse our mediocre—or worse—answers, or we justify them. Some might say, "Yeah, I can't do the things I used to, but who can at my age?" Or maybe some might say, "My dad was overweight, my mom was overweight, so I am bound to be overweight." We lose when we do this. We lose our health and we lose our dreams of vitality. Most of the time, we don't even want to get near an evaluation of our health and fitness. Most avoid getting a physical because of what may be found out. There are some people who will say, "I am in decent enough shape." Maybe they see themselves as they were on the football team or the cheerleading squad. They can't bear to admit that they have let themselves go, but they have, at least a little. All of us need a quarterly evaluation of our health and fitness, and an annual evaluation that is done by a physician and a personal trainer. Look, this is a doable thing, a winnable undertaking. Nobody is too far gone! I will talk about some simple steps to take in a bit, but for now, let's get honest.

Physical Health Assessment

Our very design is for movement. Until a little over 100 years ago, we had to trap, hunt, plant and pick, or trade for our food. We had to do it often because there were no refrigerators. We had to get it home without a car. In fact, our transportation had to be groomed, fed and cared for, which took considerable effort. Washing the clothes was more than a turn of the dial and dumping in some blue liquid, as was drying them. Everything took a lot more time and a lot more physical effort. However long you believe that man has been on this earth, we have spent the vast majority of our time being very physical. If you were out of shape you needed several kids to take care of things, otherwise you were a goner. God designed us with movement in mind.

Where are you today on a 1-10 scale? (1 is unhealthy and 10 is healthy)

- How is your health?
- What is your fitness level?
- How is your eating style?
- Where are you on the BMI index? (Google it - you will need your height and weight)
- What is your hip to waist ratio? Waist-hip ratio is calculated by dividing the measurement of your waist by the measurement of your hips. Men's ratio should be 1.0 or lower and women should be .8 or lower. So if you are a woman and have 42-inch hips and a 34-inch waist you have a healthy hip to waist ratio.

How did you do? Is there some work to do? Welcome to humanity. All of us have some work to do. Start where you are and move forward. These questions are starting points. There are more questions contained in the *TLP: Pursuing Life Workbook,* which is designed to help you live out this book. Don't be discouraged, but encouraged that you are made for change. God has built it in your bodily systems.

Aging is Not Optional, but Decaying is Optional

Aging is going to happen. From the time we are in our mid-twenties to around age thirty, we make the change and begin to lose some of our youth. Some. The speed at which we lose it is dependent on how we think and live. Again, we are not victims. Our bodies will respond to how we think and how we live so much so that we can, as Chris Crowley and Henry Lodge talk about in their book *Younger Next Year,* halt and even reverse the decaying process. Aging is not optional, but decaying is optional. In fact, 70% of what we call aging or what we attribute to aging is actually decay that is within our power to stop and reverse.[2]

For some, exercise is not a dirty word. It is something that we (yes, I said *we*) enjoy. Just last night I was asked how I can enjoy working out hard and sweating. My answer: I know what it does on the inside of me and I love when that happens. I also get the privilege to be able to out perform young people half my age, and I look pretty good too. Yet, when it is all boiled down, I want to be healthy and I know the incredible health benefit that will come through no other means is being released when I exercise.

> *Exercise is the master signaler, the agent that sets hundreds of chemical cascades in motion each time you get on that treadmill and start to sweat. It's what sets off the cycles of strengthening and repair within the muscles and joints. It's the foundation of positive brain chemistry. And it leads directly to the younger life we are promising, with its heightened immune system; its better sleep; its weight loss, insulin regulation and fat burning; its improved sexuality; its dramatic resistance to heart attack, stroke, hypertension, Alzheimer's disease, arthritis, diabetes, high cholesterol and depression. All that comes from exercise. But let your muscles sit idle and decay takes over again.*

> *Here's how it works: When your cells sense damage, say, from exercise, they automatically release chemicals to start the inflammation—to set the stage for repair. A few of those chemicals leak into the bloodstream, and those few molecules draw white blood cells to the injured area the way blood in the water draws sharks from miles around. After the inflammatory cycle has done its demolition work, the white blood cells go away, leaving behind a clean, fresh surface so the construction crews can get to work on the growth part of the cycle.[3]*

Now that is good stuff! We have amazing bodies. C-6, the chemical responsible for decay and a response to inflammation, is resident in your blood stream all the time because your cells are always dying and inflammation, even on a small level, is always happening. C-10, the chemical responsible for growth and repair, is only released when the C-6 level is high enough, which means you have to push a little in your exercising. This doesn't mean that long, slow walks have no benefit, they do; yet they will not trigger a C-10 response and that is what you need to be stronger, more fit, and to feel healthier and younger.

You may be asking what the health benefits are besides being able to lift heavier weight or ride a bike a longer distance. I'm glad you asked. Inside your blood vessels is where the C-6 and C-10 run. The leading cause of death for the last 95 years (including during WWII) is heart disease. Actually it is vascular disease, because our hearts are normally just fine. The problem comes to our hearts, or to our brains (stroke) when the blood flow gets blocked. What can you do about that? C-10. That's right, C-10 is the only thing that we know of that will actually bring healing to our blood vessels that are filled with junk from years of stress, bad eating and lack of exercise. Will it renew the walls of your arteries like those of a newborn? No, but it will bring healing and that is the point here. C-10 is for more than getting a bigger bicep. It produces health throughout your body. It is not the only thing that is turned on when you exercise, but it is a big one.

Studies have shown that our DNA changes when we exercise. What that means is that every time we put on our athletic shoes, or hiking boots, or whatever you wear on your feet when you get moving, your DNA is improving in wonderful ways. Whatever *it* may be— rowing, swimming, tennis, lifting weights or whatever—you can choose health and vitality.

Another fact to consider about decay, your muscles regenerate approximately every four months. They will adapt to whatever stress you put on them. If you are lifting weights, they will become stronger; if you are biking long distances, they will become more enduring; if you are playing tennis, they will become quicker. Our bodies will adapt to anything except a sedentary, junk food eating, isolating, pointless life. Actually they will adapt to that as well, but you won't live well for long. We are made for times of exhilaration. We are made for a challenge. Our bodies love it.

There are many things, from the Co-Q-10 enzyme (not to be confused with C-10) to HGH (human growth hormone), that decline in production as the years go by. HGH is one of those important hormones because it causes growth. Do you know there is an exercise that will raise your HGH production levels by up to 700%? High Intensity Interval Training (HIIT). It isn't an easy one, but it works! There are all kinds of benefits I could go on and on about, and I think I will in another book.

There are no age restrictions on this thing. When you are older, like in your 70s, you can still gain muscle mass, strength and endurance. Not like a 20-year-old can, but it is doable. You can develop endurance and quickness and core strength to help you live very well into you 80s and 90s, God willing. However, it is nearly magic to start in your teens and never stop. Then you will be way ahead of the people who in their 40s decided to get into shape for one reason or another, or the group in the 50s and 60s whose health necessitated exercise. This brings me to a hero of sorts in the exercise world—Jack LaLanne.

Jack LaLanne was an amazing physical specimen and he did nothing out of the ordinary. He lived a healthy lifestyle so when he was older, he could still amaze all of us.

> Age 42 (1956): Set a world record of 1,033 pushups in 23 minutes on "You Asked for It," a TV show with Art Baker.4

> Age 45 (1959): Completed 1,000 pushups and 1,000 chinups in 1 hour and 22 minutes. (Jack said this was the most difficult feat of all.)

> Age 62 (1976): Commemorating the "Spirit of '76" he swam 1 mile in Long Beach Harbor, handcuffed, shackled and towing 13 boats (representing the 13 original colonies) containing 76 people.

> Age 70 (1984): Handcuffed, shackled and fighting strong winds and currents, he towed 70 boats containing 70 people 1 ½ miles from the Queen's Way Bridge in the Long Beach Harbor to the Queen Mary.

I know how he did it. He wanted to. I know why he did it. To prove he could and to say to the generations to follow, you can do it too. Although some men and women are genetically gifted toward incredible physical feats, the message stays the same: you can be incredible.

I am not advocating that everyone be able to break those records, but to just be kinda' healthy seems like a loss. Why not aspire to greatness on some level? Whether it is being able to play ball with your grandchildren or surf with your great-grandchildren, or it is climbing 50 flights of stairs with 50 pounds and descending all within 50 minutes—just to do it. Let's do it! Let's be people who our kids talk about as being healthy, fit and strong.

> *Researchers gave 10,000 men two stress tests, five years apart. At the end of the study, the fittest men had a third the mortality of the least fit. Think about that: one-third the mortality. And even more encouraging, those who had been sedentary at the first stress test but fit by the second—those who had turned their lives around in those five years—cut their mortality roughly in half. Cut your risk of dying by half... it's hard to argue with that.[5]*

The Problem with Neglect

When you neglect yourself physically you will suffer. If you don't get enough sleep your chances to develop cancer and other diseases increase. There are consequences to our actions and Jesus isn't going to *cover* for you all the time. If you believe, like I do, that God wants us healthy and strong, and that God is our Healer, and that His ultimate design was for incredible physical prowess, then let's cooperate with God and His design. Would Jesus not rescue us? He does rescue, but whom does He rescue? When does Jesus rescue a man who has lived a life of evil? When that man surrenders to Him. If you knew somebody who gambled away all his wealth and said, "Jesus will rescue me," what would you say to him? The same thing I would say—surrender to God! So we must surrender ourselves to God who loves us, including our bodies.

The problem with neglect is it usually sneaks up on us. Let's talk weight for a moment. We all know that being overweight isn't good. In fact, it is one of the biggest contributors to disease and eventually death. However, you don't sit down at the all you can eat buffet and come out 30 pounds heavier. It happens to all of us just the same— one pound at a time. It is the small decisions to have one more...or to have desert every night, right before bed, that is sugar based! America is overweight and it is a big problem (pardon the pun).

Two-thirds of Americans are overweight and one-third of them are obese, which is a word that means really overweight. Although I am not a fan of the BMI (Body Mass Index), which is how people arrive at the numbers stated above, it only takes some simple observations in a public place to see that we have a problem with heaviness in this country.

There are a number of problems that arise from being overweight. Not the least of which are diseases that cause disabilities and death. Before we go there, we do have to define overweight. When a psychologically normal person looks in the mirror they can tell whether they are overweight or not. There are all kinds of tools that you can find online, (like the BMI index), but it really boils down to an honest evaluation of self. I am 5' 10" and weigh about 172 pounds. According to the BMI index, I am either overweight or borderline. I assure every reader, I am not overweight. Hip to waist ratio is much more indicative of health and obesity than most measurement scales.

The other question to ask is: What are we feeding ourselves? We eat whatever looks good. It is the good ol' *seefood* diet. I see it and I eat it. That reminds me of a shirt that was printed a decade ago. It said, "I don't have a drinking problem, I drink, I get drunk, I fall down, no problem." That might make some chuckle, and others would be offended. Yet that is what our diets have become. I eat whatever I want, no problem. It is a problem.

We have consumed things made in a laboratory for years. The packaged foods that can sit on a shelf for a month or two are not close to natural. They have natural pictures, but they are not natural or they would spoil just like everything else that is natural. I am not saying we all have to go 100% natural and organic (although, it's a pretty good idea), but we have to see things differently. We have become accustomed to packaged things being conveniently good, and therefore good for us. Wrong! Artificial sweeteners have fewer calories so they are good for us—wrong! They are made in a laboratory. We spray our fruit with stuff to make it pretty, we put stuff in our meats to help them keep (even though we have wonderful refrigeration and really don't need the nitrites to preserve them anymore), and we partially hydrogenate things to make them last as long as a Twinkie. (Actually longer—Twinkies are rotated out every 25 days according to reports.) Have we redefined food?

Then there is the GMO (Genetically Modified Organisms) thing. Genetically engineered seeds are taking over, literally. How unsafe are they? It isn't known yet for sure. Hey people, they are made in a lab. One thing is for sure: it isn't what God made. There are plants that when eaten by insects, the insects die. We are not insects, but doesn't it figure that there may be something in that plant that isn't good for us? There is a whole host of research and opinion about GMO, or GE foods, but suffice to say, our bodies were not created to eat them. Our bodies were created to eat the food that God created to be our food.

My mom took a popular blood sugar regulating drug. She had problems with congestive heart failure, but I figured it was because she was old. One time after a hospitalization, we brought her into our home and did some research on all her medication. We found something out that was shocking. The pill she was getting for diabetes was the probable cause of her congestive heart failure. It was the number one side effect for that particular drug. Drugs can save our lives and I am happy that we have them available. However, we medicate ourselves more than anyone in the world and most of us have no idea what we are taking. Americans consume approximately 80% of the world's medications. We have a pill for everything. Doctors now feel pressured to give antibiotics to a child whose mom brings them in for the flu. Flu is a virus and not helped by antibacterial medication. We have a problem and the problem is causing us to be a sicker nation instead of a healthier one. If you are on medications, read about them and educate yourself. Maybe you can come off them (under a doctor's care) or make a change. Find out what it is and what the side effects are; you may be surprised.

Diseases – Preventable

According to the CDC, 7 out of 10 Americans each year will die from chronic disease. Heart disease, cancer and stroke account for 50% of all deaths each year. In 2005, almost one out of every two adults had at least one chronic illness and it is rising. There are different factors like stress and the way you think, but it can all be summed up with how we live.

The top six killers in the US:

1. Heart disease – preventable
2. Cancer – most forms are preventable
3. Respiratory disease – preventable
4. Accidents – Some can be prevented
5. Alzheimer's – preventable
6. Diabetes – Type 2 or adult onset is preventable

The number one contributing factor to the above killers is being overweight and obese. Those are the serious consequences that can end our lives prematurely. When you are overweight, you are carrying more of a load than you are made to. There are other things like heightened injuries, especially to the knee joint and to the back and easy fatigue. Then there is the balance and falling issue because you can't move like you used to. On top of that there are the limitations on your movements that affect your quality of life. It is time to shed the extra pounds, one at a time.

The skinny people can have plenty of health problems as well. The way you eat has a huge effect on your health. You can look fine on the outside but be full of junk on the inside. It is very easy to identify the brain of an Alzheimer's sufferer. It has a little to do with diet but more about lifestyle and thinking. The point is that just because you are thin, doesn't mean you are healthy. In fact, the last time I saw a drug addict they were thin. Being thin is better than being overweight, but thin people, or the people in the medium size category can be extremely unhealthy as well.

When you put junk in, you have a junkie inside. The normal axiom is *garbage in, garbage out*. Not in the case of your body. Garbage in makes the inside like junk. Our bodies are magnificent and can filter out and clean up so much junk it is amazing. However, there is a limit to what we can ask our bodies to do. There really is a principle of reaping and sowing at work here. You may be able to overcome certain dietary satiations that you enjoy, but a steady diet of junk is going to harm you. There is just no doubt about that. So how much can you get away with? Bad question! Imagine an employee asking that question. "So how much sloughing off can I get away with before I get fired?" Answer: Every time you slough off, you affect the company. In this case, it is the body.

What were our bodies created to eat and drink? If you want to be in great health, eat and drink like that. Although, we do have to learn a few things, it isn't rocket science. It is the same with fitness. Our bodies were created to move, not sit inside, under artificial light, in a cubical, sitting in a chair for eight hours a day only to come home and sit some more. We were designed to move.

In *Eat That Frog!: 21 Great Ways to Stop Procrastinating and Get More Done In Less Time*, Brian Tracy says that the most successful people in business are those people who make decisions looking at the long-range implication and in view of their long-range goals.[6] Is that how we eat? Is that how we exercise? If we were planning five years or twenty years down the road, what would change? One of the keys to staying in great health is to see yourself in great health in the years and decades to come, and live on the road that will take you there. Live long range. Exercise and eat for the long range. Nobody wants to be feeble, sickly or ailing for the last 10-20 years of their lives. We don't have to! We can live like young people for a very long time.

Our bodies were created to prevent disease from taking over our life. There is a whole system created by God and designed for keeping us healthy. Please go back and re-read the words *preventable*. Some are arguing that some of these things have to do with heredity, genealogy and other factors that can't be prevented. Agreed, but it is a small percentage! The vast majority can be prevented through living a healthy lifestyle. That certainly includes keeping our immune systems functioning well.

Our immune system operates without us even thinking about it in the background of our life. However, if we think about it, it will operate with more efficiency. What I mean is that when we are purposeful about taking care of our immune system, it will function with great efficiency. Americans are literally handcuffing their immune system from functioning. With the rise of autoimmune disease and other diseases, allergies and even asthma, we have got to ask ourselves, what is happening? One of our problems is that we go to the doctor and nearly demand a pill, which almost never treats the problem. We have got to take responsibility and believe for our health and take care of our bodies.

Obesity and the Overweight Churchgoer

Several studies over the last decade, including a popular one from Northwestern University, stated that people who regularly attended church were 50% more likely to be obese. What? The church is helping put extra pounds on people? Yep. Except for Seventh-day Adventists.

It is purported that the Seventh-day Adventist community in Loma Linda, CA, has contributed to its high ranking among the healthiest people and healthiest seniors through a healthy lifestyle. The dietary norm, the higher activity levels and the sense of community all contribute to this wonderful statistic. As a Christian, I have always thought that we, the church, should lead the world in every category of life. Yet in this area, we are far behind the average American. Why?

There are no studies done on this that I could find, but I will give you some very possible reasons:

1. We do everything around food. Food and fellowship just go together, so we eat—a lot.
2. We eat horribly at those gatherings. White sugar and white flour are the most popular items, which causes weight gain and other evils in our bodies.
3. We don't place a value on our body. God does, but to us it is just not that important, not as important as other life issues.
4. Perhaps the biggest factor is we haven't submitted our eating, exercising and a few other important factors to God. We have surrendered many carnal delights—but food...we have made it acceptable to indulge.

Getting to the Next Level in Health and Fitness

(Before starting any exercise regimen or diet change, you should get your doctor's advice before beginning.)

Our bodies were created to move. These days, our problem is that we don't move much. So here we are in our sophisticated world of high tech with a dilemma. If we don't start moving we are going to die. Except our death happens slowly. Solution? Get moving!

Exercise is easier than you think and can be a lot of fun. Our problem is that we are not used to it. Once it becomes something that we do regularly, you won't be able to skip it without noticing the results. There are so many things you can do to exercise, especially if you live in a place with good climatic conditions and can get outdoors. There are gyms everywhere and not just the old standard gyms, but there are rock climbing gyms, kick boxing gyms, cross fit gyms, boot camps...and the list goes on. There are more videos than you can fit on your shelves with all kinds of different exercises focusing on different types of movements. You can jump, dance, and punch your way to health, all from your living room.

Whatever you do, just do it. Do it at least 3 times a week to start and progress until you hit 5-6 times per week. I would much prefer 6 times because that is our design, working six days and resting one. By the way, you need to rest one. In fact, your muscles need to rest for several days after a workout, which means you need to switch up your workouts. If you were weight lifting—a fantastic form of workout—you would work different muscle groups every day so the muscles can rest. Endurance training is a little different, but the same basic rest principle does apply. If you like bicycling, ride hard one day and the next day ride easier with the following day doing intervals (sprints followed by rest periods). The principle is: your muscles need recovery after a demanding workout. You have to give the C-6 and C-10 a chance to work. If you work out too hard too often, you won't get the results you are looking for.

I just trained a 58-year-old executive that hasn't worked out in years. I have him doing suspension training and walking. His schedule is crazy busy, so the schedule I gave him was to use the suspension trainer, working the upper body, twice per week. Take a walk with his wife or with one of his co-workers twice a week. Ultimately, I would like to see both of those happening 3 times per week to equal six workouts. Then we will go from there. Baby steps are best sometimes.

If you are not moving at all, start with a nice walk. Start with 15 minutes at a good pace and move it up from there. Create monthly goals of length and work up to at least 30 minutes. You can get some entry-level workout DVDs. Don't try to do P90X or Insanity right off the bat. You will be sorer than sore and there is no honor in sore. Start easy, even if you are lifting weights. I tell my trainees to lift light weights for at least two weeks just to prepare the joints, ligaments and tendons. Then increase it and lift until exhaustion after week three. If you are going to play soccer with a club, don't play the whole game, take breaks and don't play a center man who runs a lot. Injuries happen when we are doing too much, too fast. Injuries set you back and we want to avoid setbacks. Start slow and steady and work up to hard and fast.

There are some who never want to get to hard and fast. That must be in your future. Your health depends on it. Remember the lesson about the C-10? When you find something that you like to do, do it to the point where you can't hold a steady conversation with another person—your breathing needs to be about getting oxygen to your muscles and not about speaking without a little panting. Sweat too. Sweating is your body's mechanism to cool itself down. That means that you are generating heat and that is good. I am not talking about working out in the deserts when it is in triple digits; I am saying that sweating is a sign that you are working hard. Make sure to drink plenty of fluids on the days you sweat. You have to replace what is going out.

Balance Work

Balance work is really important especially as you age. Falling is to be avoided at any age, but when you are older, falling can ruin your summer or your year, and even beyond that. It can be devastating to your body. Performing exercises or activities that require balance as part of the activity is a must for everyone. I remember seeing a piece on Herschel Walker, a great NFL running back, who took ballet during his off-season. Why? Balance was one of the main reasons.

Balance training has become pretty popular. Trainers move people from a stable platform (like the floor), to unstable platforms (like a BOSU-ball) to improve the neuromuscular efficiency of the many micro muscles and stabilizer muscles throughout your body. Next time you are performing a lunge, as you come up from the lunge, raise you upper leg until it is parallel to the ground and hold it for 3 seconds, or the next time you are performing curls, do them on one leg and make sure to keep your posture straight.

Strength Training

There is no end to the benefits of strength training. You can do it with weights, machines, your own body weight, or sand bags. Any way you slice it, strength training has marvelous benefits such as building strong bones, strong connectors, burning fat (the more muscle you have the more fat you burn), and a host of other benefits, like maintaining an increased metabolic rate long after a hard work out.

A weight training regiment should start out slow and be increased incrementally. As I said before, you must spend time introducing your body to this new form of movement. Take your time. Soreness is not your trophy; it is lactic acid build up. You have to alternate days and work different muscles groups. You can work chest and back on day one, legs and abs day two, shoulders and arms day three. You should include other forms of exercise as well, such as endurance or cardio training, and that can be day four. Day five could consist of chest and back again (big muscles burn more calories), and day six do legs and abs again or, as I like to call it, core. In fact, you could add in core on several other days as well. (Remember, day seven is total rest.)

The body is adaptive and it will adapt to any training regimen. You have to change your routine every three to six weeks or you will plateau. That doesn't mean you stop working hard; instead, you can change the exercises you're doing, workout different muscles groups together, perform supersets (back-to-back exercises using the same muscles group with no rest in between), or you can certainly increase your weight (or reps) because you are getting stronger. I sometimes will insert a week or two of super-slows. Super-slows are the same or similar exercises, just done super slow, as in 15-25 seconds per repetition. That means you have to lower your weight and it is helpful to have a partner who pushes you to crank out that last repetition. That is the money repetition. Super-slows are great because they have a great result in a short amount of time. You only need to do one hard set (emphasis on *hard*) for every muscle group. Remember to always maintain great form and concentrate on using the proper muscle group rather than the synergist, or helper muscle (i.e., focus on the pectoral muscle rather than the frontal deltoid for the bench press— usually you will roll your shoulders forward to engage more deltoid). You could get a full body workout in 20-25 minutes doing super-slows and be completely fatigued if you do it right. Whatever you do, change it up and you will see more results.

Cardio (Endurance) Training

Endurance training is of the utmost importance in the health of life. This is the area when the elevators are broken, or your son or granddaughter want to hike to the falls, you will be able to make it to the top first. Cardio vascular training is so good for your system and will produce many wonderful benefits, such as lowering your blood pressure. So how do you start with this?

My preference is always outside. Do something outside. The air is better and the sun is wonderful. If you can't make that happen, then make something happen inside. Ride a bike, walk briskly, run, dance, or join a fitness class. Whatever you do, have some fun, sweat a little and do it so you can't talk comfortably. Depending on what results you want, performing a cardio workout 2-4 times per week would be good. This would give you time to recover and also keep your body in shape for the next work out. Start by increasing your heart rate to around 70% of your maximum heart rate. There are a lot of ways to figure this out, but a simple way is to take 220 and subtract your age. Multiply that number by .70 and you will have your first target. Don't go above 80% (220 − [age] x .80) until you are regularly working out for three weeks. Give your body a chance to adapt. After that point, you can have two levels of endurance training, 65-75% of your maximum heart rate and 70-85% of your max heart rate. Have some fun, punch imaginary intruders, run as if in the Olympics, or run in the mountains or on the beach and just enjoy God's creation.

Clint Gresham, long snapper for the Seattle Seahawks asked me what I try to do when I train people. One of the things I told him was that I try to train people to be in enough shape in order to perform a HIIT or Peak 8 workout. This workout, which will only take 20-25 minutes, is an incredible workout that will propel you to be in great shape. It also has the added benefit of releasing HGH (human growth hormone) in high levels. HGH is some of the magic that keeps us young and strong. Its production decreases as you age, except when you do certain forms of exercise, like HIIT. The long and the short of this workout is a 2-3 minute warm up (always followed by stretching, but not a part of the workout as it is properly termed), and then you sprint or go all out for 30 seconds and rest (walk or slow down) for the next 1 minute and 30 seconds. You cycle through that another 7 times and then you cool down for 2-3 minutes. You need to be in shape before you do this, so don't try this right out of the gate thinking that you are back on the gridiron in high school.

This is a good time to say that passing out is to be avoided. When you feel light headed or you feel like you are going to throw up, stop what you are doing! You body is signaling you that you are going too hard. You may think you are at an Olympic venue and the crowd wants to see more, but it is time to rest and reassess what you are doing. In fact, it would be wise to see a doctor at this point, especially if it has happened before. Lowering your blood pressure until passing out is not what you are after.

Core

Since recovering from back surgery, I have worked on my core like never before. I don't do endless sit-ups and crunches; that is old school. There are so many fantastic exercises to engage all your core muscles, which includes more than the rectus abdominis (the ab muscles that you see—or you want to see). Core includes your legs, butt, mid section and even some long muscles that extend all the way up your spine. Back problems are a big problem. Statistics say 60% of you will experience back pain. Be the 40% and work your core regularly. You can look up core exercise on the Internet and you will find dozens of them. As with any exercise, use good form. Tighten your buns and pull your belly button in just a little during all core exercise. This will engage the core and keep your lower back from contorting in ways that would be harmful.

Stretching

There are many opinions about stretching, but almost all agree that stretching is important. My dog gets up every morning and stretches. I didn't have to train her to do it; it came natural. We would too, except we have places to go and people to see and coffee to drink. It would be better to spend three minutes going through a little morning warm up and stretch, which would get your blood moving, loosen up your stiffness that you incurred by laying still all night, and provide full range of motion in your joints. Muscles tighten and even cramp on a fairly regular basis. We sit all day, which is shortening your hip flexors. These things will end up causing problems when we want full range of motion to play, move quick or even shower.

There is another reason that stretching and massage (you can thank me later) is really important. We develop small cramps in our muscle fiber. If those knots aren't worked out through stretching or massage, a non-elastic collagen mass will form, which will limit future muscle elasticity and therefore affect joint range of motion. If there is one thing you don't want it is partial range of motion.

One thing worth mentioning here is, do not stretch a cold body. Warm up a little, get the blood flowing and then stretch. There are a few different types of stretching and here is a good run down:

Static

This is the standard form or stretching that we have been using forever. Usually held for 10 seconds, it really is more useful to hold for 30 seconds. A 30 second hold allows for the muscle to relax and stretch a bit more. One thing I want to mention here: forcing the muscle to stretch is dangerous and can end up tearing muscle fibers or worse, tearing tendon and ligaments fibers. Don't have someone stretch you to the point of pain. A little discomfort is fine, but not pain.

Ballistic

This form of stretching uses momentum to stretch further. Where it would be bouncing or hugging yourself like a swimmer before a race, momentum is used to stretch further than you would without the momentum. This type of stretching has to be used with caution because you can injure yourself by forcing the muscle to go further than it wants to.

Dynamic

Dynamic is similar to ballistic but it uses the opposite muscle contraction to stretch the antagonist muscles. These movements are not held or bounced. They go to a certain point and then return. Running in place with high knees is actually stretching your glutes (butt muscles) while contracting your abs and hip flexors. This is a good way to warm up and stretch out.

Active Isolated Stretching

Also called A.I.S. is becoming the favorite method of stretching because of its results and lack of down sides. This is performed by stretching your muscles to the end of its stretching point and holding for 2 seconds and then returning to neutral. Then you repeat that 6-8 times and each time you can stretch just a little more. This is a terrific way to stretch that can be utilized before your workout.

Self-Myofascial Release

This is rolling your body on a hard cylinder of foam, otherwise called foam rolling. This is a fantastic thing to do at home if you are just kicking back or watching TV. The only thing that works out the knots better is a massage. As you are rolling your body on this, when you feel a twinge of pain, maybe a knot, stop there and hold it for 30 seconds. Keep rolling around and find those knots and hold it for their release.

One more thing about stretching: It is my opinion that the lean over and touch your toes hamstring stretch isn't good for people with back issues and may not be good for your back at all. Some preliminary studies have shown this, but the jury is still out, except for me. Instead of stretching down, stretch out by bending at the waist and extending your arms straight ahead. Better yet, get a partner to stretch you on the ground. This is accomplished by laying flat on your back with your legs out straight and a partner lifting one straight leg while the other stays on the floor. Also, a little trick is if you tense up and push a little against your friend with the raised leg and then relax, you will be able to stretch just a little more. Remember: do not stretch to the point of pain.

Moving in the Workplace

It takes a lot of physical work to put up a high-rise or low-rise office building, but those who work inside are desk sitters by and large—this is dangerous. There was an article published by the Mayo Clinic in January entitled "Why Sitting is the New Smoking." The basic findings of their study were that sitting all day in an office type job was as harmful to your health as smoking cigarettes. Disease, weight gain, and more come along with a desk job, not to mention things like carpel tunnel and low back issues. What to do? Get moving!

- Why not go for a short walk during lunch? Get outside and get some fresh air. If the air is 30 degrees, then walk somewhere inside or do some walking lunges. Sure, people may look at you funny, but soon they will be looking at you with jealousy because you make it look easy.
- Some offices are engineering their desks with treadmills so they can walk while they work. That is a bit expensive, so how about an exercise ball? You can burn an extra 100-300 calories a day on those things and you will strengthen you core muscles and posture, provided you sit properly on it.
- Get up and do some chair squats. With proper form, put your chair on its lowest position and stand up and sit down. Do it 15-20 times every hour or so.
- Get a smaller water cup and get up every hour to fill it.
- Stand up and move things from one side of your desk to another and then back again 10 times.

Find something that gets you moving; increased oxygen means increased thinking capacity.

Intake

Eating styles are varied, but for far too many people eating includes whatever is easy, or cheap, or quick; or it's eat whatever I want. Dangerous. We have all been on the *seefood* diet (whatever I see, I eat) and we have laughed about it. The reality is that diets are dumb for the most part and I'll tell you why. When you are off whatever diet, whether it is valuable, good for you, or scientifically proven or not, you go back to eating the way you used to, which is what got you into trouble in the first place.

I would like to introduce a concept that I call lifestyle eating. Lifestyle eating is eating for the lifestyle you want. I want to be vibrant, healthy, strong, fast, and when I get old (I am only 52 now) I want to be all of these things. So I am going to eat like I want to live.

Let's say I wanted to gain about 40 pounds and become generally unhealthy, then I would eat whatever I could find that would put weight on me. Sugar cereal in the morning, fast food in the afternoon and something from a box at night—ridiculous, right? Not really. We eat how we will live. It is the floating down the river syndrome all over again. Just put the food in my mouth and hope it helps. Praying over it helps, right? (Have I gone too far?) No. This is the last thing to be surrendered to God's plan for most people. We eat what tastes good and what tastes good is sugar stuff! (Or, if you are like me, fried and salted stuff). There is a price that nobody wants to pay. Yet changing is easier than we think.

Start with some baby steps here. You don't have to go all organic and grass fed, just take some good steps. Get rid of the high fructose corn syrup (well, there goes my Coke endorsement). Stop eating anything that is hydrogenated or partially hydrogenated. Read the labels. You will find out that so many things have sugar in them; it will make you mad. Food producers know something: sugar keeps you coming back for more.

If you want to eat healthier to live healthier, eat more wholesome foods, the closer to the ground the better and the fewer ingredients the better. I held up a bag or nacho Doritos and listed off over thirty ingredients. Not all were bad ingredients, but there were over *thirty*. Then I held up a bag of TJ's Organic Corn Chips, which had only *three* ingredients. I am not saying to eat fried corn chips, but if you are going to consume chips, get the ones with three ingredients. If it is processed, then the best stuff in the food has been nearly taken out. Don't you wonder why they "enrich" some foods? Because they depleted the food of its nutrients in the processing.

Portion control is a huge issue and I can't tell you how much to eat or even how many calories, but I can tell you this, when you are full stop eating. If we would eat slower, chew well and exercise, then our bodies would tell us enough already. Unless you are an athlete or you are working out hard and long, you don't need seconds or huge portions. TGIF (Fridays restaurant) offers menu items that are smaller portions. I have no idea about their healthiness, but most portions in restaurants are more than we need. If we would have a bit more protein in our diets, we would eat less, because protein is more satiating than carbs.

Speaking of proteins and carbs… as far as being overweight goes, carbs are the culprit. Carbohydrates are needed for life. Every cell's energy comes from them. If you don't eat carbs then your body breaks down fat and turns them into carbs. (Not actually carbs, I am just putting it in simple terms, it is actually ketones). So carbohydrates are not bad, they are essential to life. They power your brain. You need them. People are just consuming so much more than they need. So when the body gets more energy (carbs) than it needs, it stores it as fat. Our bodies are then supposed to draw from the fat storage (the quick fat storage is right around the mid section) and utilize it for energy since we are consuming energy all the time. So if you take in more energy than you burn and your stores are already full, you build more stores so to speak. People have tried to cut down on their fat intake thinking that is what was making them fat. Nope. It is the flour and the sugar and the starches that we consume in such high quantity. As a matter of fact, our bodies need fat. It is a necessity. Unsaturated fat and the highly contested saturated fat are essential for the maintaining of proper health and the building of nearly every cell in your body.

There are some popular and effective weight loss diets that reduce or eliminate carbs. This too can be dangerous if done for any length of time. (There goes my Paleo endorsement.) Protein can be used for energy and the bi-product of the deamination process (the process by which amino acids are broken down to be used for energy) is a toxic substance, ammonia. But so is the waste from the explosion of the glycogen molecule. The point is that this diet, like others, is not life sustaining. One just has to think about the original creation and God's intention, which was all the stuff that grows out of the earth and later included certain animals, and you can envision the type of eating style that we should have if we want great health. Certain diets will help you lose weight (who wants to be skinny and sickly?), but they won't improve health, which is our ultimate goal.

Overall we eat to live; not live to eat. To eat is to get the fuel and the nutrients that we need in order to live. The more color in your food (natural color) the better. There is so much more to fruits and vegetables than vitamins, things like phytonutrients and trace minerals that mean so much to our bodies. You get those through good food sources and good supplements.

Supplements

Do you need them? Probably. From the soil, to the plants, to the early picking of the fruit, our food just doesn't have the nutrient value it used to, not to mention the hybridization and the genetic modification of our plants. Good supplement sources are also food based. Factory created (synthetic) vitamins and supplements are not great since they are not from God's creation. The best supplements are those that are natural, or as close as possible to natural. Your body is made to assimilate natural things.

Most of us are deficient in many vitamins and minerals not to mention essential fatty acids. One way to tell is to get a blood test from a good doctor that is nutritionally minded. There are also other ways to test or discern if you are deficient in certain things. There are some good people out there that are dedicated to helping you gain health without medication, and there are good resources you can find to help you as well. You will have to do some legwork on this, but here is a list of some supplements that most people need.

Multivitamins and Minerals

If it is all in one pill, it is not enough. It is impossible to pack all the needed nutrients into one pill. The normal dose should be three or more tablets per day. If you can get it in liquid form, all the better.

B-Complex Vitamins

Most of us are deficient for a number of reasons in our B vitamins, which are essential for many reasons, including energy.

Omega-3s

Good quality fish oil supplements will give you a boost in omega-3 fatty acids. You will have to research to find a good source.

Protein Supplements

Whey protein is the accepted standard, but again, it is the source that matters. You have to do your research on the company that makes the supplements. How much protein do you need? If you want to build muscle, then you will need to increase your protein intake. There is a lot of information on how many grams you need, but here is one tip: drink or eat a high protein meal or shake within an hour of your workout. This will help in the protein synthesis of your muscles. If you are a vegetarian, there are good plant source proteins available. I am not a fan of soy because of the phytoestrogen in the plant. Vegetarians, in most cases, need to supplement protein to maintain or grow their muscle mass.

Calories

Everyone wants to know how many calories they should be taking in per day. There are plenty of apps and programs that estimate that based on certain factors. The real answer is that if you eat to live, then you will eat when you need to. If you are an athlete, you eat way more than an accountant that walks three times per week. I have known some NFL players and they have to eat like a horse to keep their weight up. If you are a triathlete, you are going to consume double or triple what a normal person consumes. There are no magic numbers here. Remember that all the graphs and scales and opinions are generalized for the masses to have some kind of index to look at. It isn't an individualized science. You have to set your intake by recognizing what you need. That comes from paying attention to your body.

When is a calorie not a calorie? When it has a balanced glycemic index. In other words, you can eat more calories when you have a diet with balanced glycemic levels than when you don't. There are smart ways of eating and one of them is to have protein with your carbs and don't peel the skin off anything, it is there for a reason. It either slows down absorption, or it contains fiber, or it has another benefit. If you have to have toast with jelly (not a recommended breakfast), then put some wholesome, no sugar added peanut butter, or better yet almond butter on it too.

Water

Drink plenty of water. Notice that I didn't say iced tea or soda; I said water. You need to be drinking up to about half your body weight in ounces daily as a minimum. Less than 64 oz. per day and you will most likely be in a state of dehydration. Water has great benefits such as:

- It flushes toxins.
- More water = less water weight.
- It keeps your metabolism up.
- It can keep you from over eating, or eating when you aren't hungry. You know those middle-of-the-day, just-ate-not-too-long-ago hunger signs? You are most likely dehydrated and your body is mixing up the thirst and hunger signals.
- You will have clearer skin, less muscle soreness, sleep better and allow your body to function properly.

Sunlight

This is a touchy subject because we have heard for years that you will get skin cancer if you go in the sun. I am not saying to go out until your skin is fried. Do not over do it. However, you need to get into the sun. Our skin produces Vitamin D when we are exposed to the sun's Ultraviolet B rays. It really is quite an amazing thing. All we need is 15-20 minutes per day on our forearms and we will have enough. Vitamin D is an amazing substance with a receptor in just about every cell in your body. In other words, vitamin D is essential. It is probably one of the greatest cancer fighting substances we have found. You can take it orally, but you need the right kind and you need a fair amount of it. The sun is the best provider.

Touch

We are born with an intense skin hunger. Babies have a deep need for touch, and if not forthcoming, healthy development is hindered. Touch is a God-given need. Touch has actual physiological effects on our biochemical and bioenergetics systems. Brain wave activity is increased, resulting in better alertness for instance. The amount of insulin needed in diabetics is reduced, hormone levels increase and sleep patterns are enhanced. Touch is physically necessary and beneficial to our entire sense of well being. Through touch multiple neuronal messages are transmitted to our brains stimulating the production of hormones (chemical/emotional energy) that provide physical and emotional good feelings. Simply put, humans thrive on touch.

I read of a study where rabbits were stacked in cages up to the ceiling. They were being jammed full of cholesterol or something to study plaque buildup, but there were some abnormal results. The rabbits in the lower tiers did much better than the ones up high. It turns out the lab person, who was short, loved animals. She patted and fussed over the ones she could reach, which had 60% less plaque than the ones up high. The scientists swapped the rabbits around, high for low. And the ones that were now reachable also prospered. It was the patting and touching, no question about it.

Rest

We need it! We are overworked and over stimulated to the point of sleep deprivation. In a dark and quiet room, how long would it take you to fall asleep? If you are like most westerners it would take you a couple of minutes or less, which means you are sleep deprived (it should take about 10-20 minutes to fall asleep). We need our body to recalibrate and recover from the day. Lots of building is going on in the body as well as rest for some vital organs. How much sleep we need is hotly contested, but the people who say they feel fine on five hours are being deceived. A sleep cycle is generally 1 ½ hours and you could use six of them. That's 9 hours. So you can't spend that much time resting your body? Then get 7 ½ hours at a minimum. You can't cheat your sleep and not suffer the consequences. Who wants to be tired anyway? Get some sleep. Arrange your life to live it to the full, which includes at least five sleep cycles.

Down Time

You physical and mental body needs down time. The Jews called it a Sabbath. God actually instituted this rest day. He also made the sun go down to signal the end of something—the day. We seem to have been able to circumvent both. Enjoy your life, slow down, take a day off and live better. You will function better, be happier and more productive if you take time off. Your body and brain need it.

Laughing

> A cheerful heart is good medicine, but a crushed spirit dries up the bones. (Proverbs 17:22)

Laughter releases an instant flood of feel-good chemicals that boost the immune system and almost instantly reduce levels of stress hormones. For example, a really good belly laugh can make cortisol drop by 39% and adrenalin by 70%, while the feel-good hormone (endorphin) increases by 29%. It can even make growth hormones skyrocket by 87%! Other research shows how laughter boosts your immune system by increasing immunity levels and disease-fighting cells.

Laughter protects your heart, because when you laugh and enjoy yourself, your body releases chemicals that improve the function of blood vessels and increase blood flow, protecting against heart attack. Fun reduces damaging stress chemicals quickly, which, if they hang around in your body for too long, will make you mentally and physically sick. Fun and laughter also increase your energy levels. Laughing is good for the soul and the body. So laugh. Get a dog, get around a 2-year-old, watch America's Funniest Videos, do something to laugh. Do it often.

Injuries and Disabilities

If you are injured or disabled somehow and have physical limitations, then you have to work with them, not live defeated. Again, you need to check with your doctor before starting an exercise program, but don't let things hold you back. You have to work around them. I have had injuries and surgeries that have altered what I do. However, they didn't stop me all together. That has got to be your mentality. I know a man who is wheel chair bound with Muscular Dystrophy who works out with a personal trainer 2-3 times per week. This guy is in his 60s and isn't going to let this horrible disease stop him from fighting for the best health he can maintain. You are a champion Dr. John. I admire you!

Aging Well

Ending well on this earth is what all of us desire. Not one of us wants to be pushed around in a chair or need a walker. None of us wants to lose function because of stroke or other diseases. We want to end vital and full of life. It is possible. Moses did it, Joshua did it, I am going to do it, and you can do it too. Be purposeful about your life, how you live, and continue to ask for and receive God's blessing of health. Don't wait until you have something wrong to do the right things so you can get a better outcome. Do the right things now;

choose life now, and you will live to your maximum. This isn't about beating anybody else in life; this is about being the best *you* that you can be. Then when you have decided that, take it up to the next level and believe God for greater results than you could have brought on your own.

Create some goals and make a plan. Start slow and make attainable goals. Show your plan to others. Get someone that has a similar plan to join you. Carry out your plan. After you have carried it out for a while, revise it and shoot for a higher goal. Get my *TLP: Pursuing Life Workbook* and keep track of the institution of your plan and your goals. Whatever you do, write it down and let your progress encourage you to keep going. You can do this. God is with you.

7

Mental Part of the Whole

- Research has indicated that people who have healthy attitudes about aging instead of toxic, negative ones live 7.5 years longer![1]
- High stress levels (which are the result of poisonous, toxic thoughts) suck biochemical resources away from cell repair and kill brain cells.[2]
- One nerve cell grows 15,000 to 200,000 branches, about the amount of facts learned in one 12th grade subject.
- You have enough brain cells to accumulate and store over 3 million years worth of information.
- Emotions are chemicals within the thought structures of your brain that send messages throughout your body. The famous neurological researcher Candice Pert once said, "Even your big toe knows you are angry."
- You have 24-48 hours to either accept (passively or actively), or reject a thought before it becomes an actual physical structure in your brain.
- The unconscious mind has 4000 processes per second.
- The conscious mind has 2000 processes per second.
- Studies say that 75-98% of non-viral/bacterial psychological and physical maladies are a result of your thought life.[3]

- Negative thoughts lower dopamine levels (the chemical in the brain associated with pleasure and reward), and release proteins that create negative influences in your brain.
- Every time you laugh your brain releases chemicals that prepare it for learning.
- Thinking hateful thoughts tightens your DNA. It also releases hundreds of chemicals into your bloodstream, whereas within 10-30 seconds of thinking loving thoughts your DNA relaxes.[4]

Amazing, huh? Our brains are wonderful and the research has only begun to unveil the incredible ability of the human being. When thinking about the significance of the mental area of life, our thought life, I already knew that we could improve our intellect. I knew we could improve our memory. I knew about the renewing of the mind. I knew that we could choose to think the way we want to think, but I never understood the truly amazing and awesome ability of our brain.

"You are a neuroplastician." That is the phrase that caught my attention during a seminar led by Dr. Caroline Leaf. I hadn't decided what direction to take about the mental area of life. There were so many things I could encourage people to do to improve themselves mentally, but on this day, a whole new world opened up. Since then I have been on a journey to learn and understand our amazing brains.

I spent three days alongside 80-100 people listening to Dr. Leaf explain things about our brains in ways that made me want to know more. That is the mark of a great teacher. My eyes opened to the possibility that there were answers for people that really struggle with the way they think. I also learned about how much control we have over our mental health and the way we think. We don't have to settle for some kind of malfunction of the brain or be victimized by the way we think. The chemical inadequacies that plague us can be brought to normal. Chemical imbalance, negative thought cycles (or circuits), and a host of organic as well as inorganic problems can be healed.

Our minds and our brains are created to be great. They were created to love. They were created to be positive. We are designed for deep intellectual thought. We are designed to learn and grow in intellect. God created intelligent people to communicate with Him. We can be in homeostasis (balance) and operate as we were meant to operate. Am I saying that we can be 100% just like Adam, the perfect man, or Eve, the perfect woman? No, but how about in the 90s? I think most have settled to operate far below our capacity. We were created to operate at maximum efficiency. If that was God's intention from the beginning, then He will help you get there.

Before we go any further, there are two concepts that we need to cover. The first is to define the mind-brain connection. The second is the concept that I mentioned from Dr. Leaf's seminar: neuroplasticity.

Many people wouldn't think much about the difference between the *mind* and the *brain*, but there is a difference. My point here is not to give a long theological, philosophical or physiological dissertation, but you need to understand where I am coming from in my approach to the mind and the brain. Let's start with the brain.

The Brain

The brain is that thing in your skull. It is 100% organic material and it is connected to all of you. If it stops working, your body dies. Your brain can grow, change shape and has the ability to be toxic, but it is predisposed to balance (homeostasis) and positivity. You may be thinking, you don't know my husband, he is anything but positive. That is his choice (which has to do with the mind), mixed with his upbringing (the sensitivity of the brain in the early years cannot be overstated), his own life choices and genetics (somewhere from 2-20% of how we operate is genetic).

The Mind

The mind is something that is a little more difficult to define. The Merriam-Webster online dictionary defines it as:

1:   *Recollection, memory*
2:   *a: the element or complex of elements in an individual that feels, perceives, thinks, wills, and especially reasons*
        b: the conscious mental events and capabilities in an organism
        c: the organized conscious and unconscious adaptive mental activity of an organism[5]

In Jewish thought, abstractly the mind was the totality of man's inner or immaterial nature. It is closely associated with the heart, and funny enough, science bears out a brain-heart connection that is incredible. In Greek thought, the mind is more about intellect and thinking capacity. So whether you are going with the Jew or the Greek, the mind is immaterial. The American version is less parsed and seems to lean toward the mind being immaterial. The mind is the part of us that cannot be held in the hand or contained in the skull. Our minds are a part of our souls.

This matters because I believe that the mind controls the brain and not the reverse. The reason that this needs to be said is that we humans have created godless philosophies that have left our life to chance. If our brains control our reasoning, thinking, attitude and will, then we are victims to genetics, epigenetics, upbringing, sociology and so on. We are not victims! The IQ movement was born out of the behaviorist movement and has the belief that we are machines and endeavored to put us in a box that can't change. Personality profiles try to fit people into a limited number of boxes that can't change. That is why we are a blend of Marston's DISC assessment, or a Myers-Briggs test, or any other theory that tries to describe our personality. We have tendencies, but those can change with maturity. Our minds control our brains, and therefore, we are in control. Let's make this simple application; we are not victims of our biology. We can change.

Neuroplasticity

This is the term that is used to articulate our ability to form physical thought structures. Your brain is made up of many components: the cortex, the amygdala, the hypothalamus and much more, not to mention over 100 billion nerve cells. The popularization of neuroplastiticity happened in the mid 1990s when scientists discovered that we could grow our brains. People who had brain injuries were able to overcome them by growing other neurons and neural connectors to compensate for the injured portion of the brain. This has developed into the understanding that we can grow our brains by the way we think. So if you think negatively, you will grow negative dendrites. (Think of dendrites as little thought structures in your brain that look like small trees.) If you think positive, you will grow positive. For example, if you associate a scripture with a thought, you can grow a neural pathway from one thought (the scripture) to the other thought (maybe a life philosophy). This is an incredible breakthrough of understanding, which again validates what the Bible has said all along. It tells us that our minds can be renewed (Romans 12:2). If your thinking is renewed, your brain will be renewed and your normal operational mode will change. Therefore, you are a neuroplastician and you can shape your brain by the way you think.

This is bigger news than you may think because this means that you can change the thought structures that have been in your brain by what you thought was written in permanent marker. When you believe something, or ascertain knowledge, or have an experience a structure is built in your brain that is called a dendrite. Think of it like a plant or a small tree. That plant contains the information that you learned. You could have learned how to swim, or how to multiply fractions, or that your wife doesn't like how the color light blue looks on her; whatever it is, when you learn it and accept it, it begins to grow as an actual structure (think plant) inside of your head. The down side to this is that you accepted that you were fat and were told so in school, or that you were lazy, or that you couldn't perform in certain ways or that you would be a failure. Maybe you have even told yourself that. That builds a structure too. Whatever you accept as fact, along with your experiences, builds a structure in your brain. These structures are your memories and they have chemicals attached to them that we call emotions. So good or bad, they are there and you built them. When they are good plants (dendrites), all is well and life is good. When they are bad or erroneous, then we are in trouble with the way we process life.

When we have these bad or toxic dendrites, the negative, pessimistic and outright lies that we have accepted about ourselves, others and life they mess us up. Not only is there wrong thinking there, but there is bad juice that is delivered from the wrong thinking. What I mean is that negative thinking produces chemical imbalances, specifically certain proteins, which produce more chemical imbalances. Your brain has over 100 known chemicals and negative thinking upsets the balance and even releases chemicals that injure brain cells. How important is our thinking? How important is the way we talk to others and especially to our children? This is incredible stuff.

So it follows that when we are stressed out we release all kinds of chemicals that cause chain reactions throughout your brain and body. Then we have cortisol and adrenaline (epinephrine) flowing through our brain and body. They are good secretions of the adrenal glands, however, if they are too constant (in other words, if you are stressed out for long periods of time or very often) they become a negative influence instead of a positive one. That is the problem with brain chemicals, they all need to be in just the right amount or they become a problem. The problems with this are many, but one large issue of our brain is that when it is overloaded on these two chemicals, because they are constantly flowing, it messes up the circuitry and causes the switches between organs—that should be cycling on and off—to get stuck in the on position, which in turn causes more imbalances in your brain chemicals, and here we go again. For instance, the hypothalamus is the response mechanism that gets the stress hormone flowing by dropping CRS to the pituitary, which drops ACTH to the adrenals. The adrenal gland secrets epinephrine and cortisol, which bathes the pituitary and hypothalamus, which will stop them from flowing; however, when you have toxic thinking the hypothalamus and pituitary never stop flowing and you have too much CRS and ACTH. It is a chemical circuit that causes an overload and the effect is to release more, which is too much.

Stress also has an effect on happy messengers, the chemicals like GABA that carry good feelings. It depletes them. As if that weren't enough, stress hormones basically block the loading docks so that the happy messengers can't unload their good feelings. (You are getting the picture.) Stress, on an ongoing basis, is a problem for your brain and it actually alters the way you think and feel.

Here is the good news. Since we are neuroplasticians, we can grow our brain, right? That means you can actually and physically replace bad thoughts with good thoughts, wrong thoughts with right thoughts, and ungodly thoughts with Godly thoughts. Let's say that you were told you were dumb in school. Even your parents called you their "little dumb head" as some kind of pet name. You received it and it grew. Now you are 25 and still have the idea that you are dumb stuck in your head. You filter everything through that. It could define you or it could hinder you, but you can't shake it. When the chips are down and things fall apart, you play the dumb head card. The good news is you can replace it. Just like the Bible says, you can renew your mind.

As I mentioned above, if you think a thought and believe it, it produces a structure in your brain. Thinking deeply is essential for this process and we will talk about that a little later. When you think, "I am smart," and "I am well able to mentally handle...," you will begin to replace the negative dendrite (little tree) with a positive one. How science believes it works is as your new thought is growing, the old thought is dying. Soon the healthy, positive plant is in the place of the dead plant, which has evaporated into heat (because it is an actual physical structure, it has to go somewhere). The thought, "I am dumb," is now out of your filtering mechanism and the new, "I am smart," thought has replaced it. The frontal lobe of the brain analyses the decision you're considering and draws on the Scripture that you've memorized and activates it, bringing it to bear on the decision. As something comes into the conscious mind, it becomes malleable, for about 10 minutes or so. For 10 minutes we need to apply God's Truth, apply faith and apply hope to the decision we're going to make. The good thoughts will literally shoot electromagnetic forces destroying the toxic branches weakening the connections of the toxic thoughts. The chemicals released melt away the branches. Those bad, negative branches will eventually be completely melted down and will disappear.

I don't know about you, but this brings massive amount of hope to me. I grew up in a negative atmosphere in which my mom regularly told me that I couldn't do this or that. I am not a victim to that upbringing or thinking. I can change it if I want to and so can you. What is it for you? What was ingrained in you since an early age? What has stuck with you all these years? What have you repeated over and over again to yourself? You can change my friend. You can change.

Genetics

I said before that genetics figure in to who we are to the tune of 2-20%. Here again is the good news: we have the ability to override our genetic predispositions as they have been called. You can't physically change your eye color, but you can overcome the predisposition to be angry or to worry that came to you via a genetic code.

Epigenomes are those genetic markers that have been passed down to us through our parents. They are thought to carry certain personality characteristics that will predispose us to certain behaviors. These epigenomes must be activated in order to have an affect on us. Many times they are activated through stress or chemicals that we consume. These genes do not cause behavior, but rather give us certain tendencies to behave in particular ways, but your genes do not have the final say...you do. The good news is we have the power to deactivate them as well. It is our choice and that is why we can't say that we got this from our parents. We can reject these predispositions even after we have activated its genetic expression. Say good-bye to some old friends that have gotten you into trouble time and time again.

Food and the Brain

So far, I have talked about cellular level stuff—neurons, and the like. This is where the small amount of bad stuff we ingest gets to be a problem. When we eat foods with pesticides or additives, it does affect our cells. When our cells are affected, our health is affected. How much it affects us is up for debate, but by our discussion about the brain, I think you can see how important it is to not only to think right but also to consume the correct things for our bodies as well as our brains. For example, besides oxygen your brain needs proteins. Low protein diets are a problem if you want to think correctly. Your brain is 80% fat so you need fat, especially essential fatty acids. Your brain needs energy, so it needs glucose, which comes from carbohydrates. I am not saying table sugar should be used, but natural sugar (simple carbs) found in nature as well as complex carbs, which are found in foods like steel cut oatmeal (a great breakfast food) and other whole grain foods. Too much sugar produces an altered effect and throws your brain chemistry out of balance. We haven't even begun to discuss hormones, I'll save that for another book, but those things are powerful and if you are not secreting the right amounts, you are in trouble. We need to care deeply about what goes in our mouth (and our ears and even our eyes), let alone what kind of thoughts roll around in our brains.

There are foods and nutrients that really help the brain to function well. Wild Salmon, avocados, blueberries, nuts and seeds are among the foods that help brain health through their nutritional value. (That is why we eat, right? For the nutritional value of food? I digress.) Iron is an important substance because it is a transporter of sorts. Women are especially susceptible to anemia and should get tested regularly. Anemia will not only result in body fatigue, but brain fatigue.

There are two more nutrients that I have read about, folic acid and B12 that can aid in maintaining brain volume and decreasing brain health. Folic acid is super important for gestating mothers, however it also aids in decreasing brain age. In my research I read about a study where the difference in the folic acid takers and the placebo takers after three years was a five-year reduction in brain age. When you start to research how to keep your brain young, you will be amazed at how many helpful things you can consume that are easily assimilated into your life, like taking folic acid and B12 supplements or eating foods like beans and dark leafy vegetables that are high in folic acid. I must warn you here that you can eat right, but if you don't think right, you are still working against yourself. We have to bring ourselves into harmony. What we think, with what we eat, with how we love....

Exercise

I talked plenty about exercise in the Physical Part of the Whole chapter, but let me give you a few wonderful benefits to the brain by simple exercise. Movement produces blood flow. Blood has all the stuff that the brain needs. That is why John Medina, author of Brain Rules, says that if there is a magic bullet for brain health and function, it is exercise. Research shows that children who exercise before a test (within 30 minutes) increase a full letter grade on average. There have been tests conducted on the elderly who are experiencing dementia or Alzheimer's that show they are more lucid after exercise. Nothing is a magic fixer, but exercise boasts wonderful benefits including

95

endorphin release that tells your brain that things are good. It reduces bad chemicals and can bring the open circuit of dumping chemicals into your system to a close, or at least reduce the chemicals.

Sleep and the Brain

In 1995, a NASA study found that a "26-minute nap improved performance 34% and alertness 54%."[6] That is nothing to wink at. Sleep is powerful for the brain. We laugh or scoff at people who need a nap in the middle of the day, but the reality is that they will perform better mentally because of it.

We don't know everything that goes on during sleep in our brain, but what we do know is more could be going on during sleep than when we are awake. The brain is basically filing the information absorbed from the day. That is why your memory and your learning function is better after a good nights sleep. So forget pulling the all-nighter studying, get some sleep and you will do better on the test. Deep sleep helps you grow your neuro connectors. They grow best in deep sleep. Sleep is not optional for your brain. In fact, without it, you will go crazy. Sleep problems are associated with nearly every psychological problem. I talked about how much you need to sleep in the Physical Part of the Whole chapter.

Your Uniqueness

One of society's problems is conformity. Even the hippies (and now the hipsters) conform to the standard of hippie or hipster. It is hard to get away from. Nearly every school has the same strategy for learning: sit down, be quiet, listen to me, look up here, now write, a lot. Be quiet while you do your work and don't ask me to go to the bathroom again. Then go home and write more. Some school children have the workload of a CEO, but they are only eight years old. Not everybody does well in school. Take the top 10 inventors in history and you will find most, if not all of them, were not good students and some, like Edison, didn't finish. Why? They were unique. So are you.

Everyone processes differently. How you process is how God made you. The trick is to not try to process like Sam or Sally or whoever else, but to process like you. Men and women are different and they process things differently. I know I just amazed you with my knowledge, but if you believe that is true, why do we want our spouse to process like we do? We all learn differently, we view things differently, we see things differently and thoughts go screaming fast through our brain differently, which makes us unique. How our brains work is our unique fingerprint, our DNA. You have got to make it work for you.

"Scientists have found that the non-conscious mind performs around 400 billion actions per second and the conscious mind is only aware of 2000 bits of information. So there is an enormous amount of exceptionally high-speed things going on in our minds as we think through our gift processing information."[7] Based on the Dr. Caroline Leaf's Geodesic Information Process Theory, your thoughts move from the basal forebrain to each of the seven parts and depending on your profile and uniqueness you may stay longer in different areas. The entire process takes two seconds and scientists can't figure out your unique blueprint of operations with our current technology. (We have seven areas to our brains and we bring all seven areas to the table with every decision.)[8] As you approach transformation and neuroplasticity, you have to approach it your own unique way. It's okay to be you. Celebrate it.

Renewing Your Mind

I think we have established that the way we think matters. Positive or negative, you get to choose. It's like this story of a dog and cat. The dog's favorite thing is waking up, and then it is going for a walk, and then it is eating, and then it is running around, and then it is greeting the kid's coming home from school or the master getting home from work. Then its favorite thing is eating dinner and taking a nap, then it is watching TV with humans and then it is going to sleep. However a cat wakes up and thinks, "This is my 998th day of captivity!" You can choose which way you will live.

Do not conform any longer to the pattern of this world, but be transformed by the renewing of your mind. Then you will be able to test and approve what God's will is—his good, pleasing and perfect will. (Romans 12:2)

In Ephesians, Paul tells us to "be renewed in the spirit of your mind" (Ephesians 4:23 NKJV), and in Colossians the call is to be "...renewed in knowledge according to the image of Him who created him (Colossians 3:10 NKJV). There is a lot of renewing that needs to go on and it is going to take purposeful effort on our part. Remember that change happens when we apply strength and effort to our choice. This is no different. Most of life is a partnership with God. The spiritual pixie dust (wherever they might use that), just doesn't work. Things are made new when we come to Christ—like our heart—but it's like there is old DNA that flows through the new heart and infects it. We give our lives to God and He gives us His strength to cooperate with Him to bring about change in us. This is especially true in the area of thinking, which could be called the greatest battleground. We get to think how we want to, but even then it takes work to be renewed. Thank God it is not impossible, nothing is with God on our side. You can do this. Transformation is waiting.

James talks about "the implanted Word [of God]" (James 1:21 NKJV). We need to memorize Scripture in order to build those healthy branches that your brain will draw on during the decision-making process. I will go one step further than this, which is especially important since the west stops with memorization. We need to meditate on God's Words. Meditation as you will see, is the most secure way for your thinking, thought life and dendrites to change. It is a generally accepted fact that it takes 21 days to build a new habit or to get rid of an old one. That means it takes 21 days to renew your mind. Wouldn't it be nice if we could renew our mind all at once, but that would be like you personally cutting down every tree in Yellowstone National Park (3468 sq. miles) in 21 days and replanting seedlings. However, you could cut down one tree at a time, cut it up, get the stump out and replace that with a seedling. (I am not saying we should cut down trees in Yellowstone, it is just an illustration.) One thought at a time may seem like it will take a lifetime, and it will for the most part. However, there are some predominate thoughts that stand in your way of positive thinking, accelerated living, Godly thinking, or whatever you want to call it. You probably have three to twelve foundational life thoughts or philosophies that need direct attention. Based on those thoughts (structures in your brain), you have many more subordinate thoughts that you will have to deal with as well. When you get those core foundational thoughts corrected, you change the "I am dumb," to "I am smart and well able," and you will reap huge dividends. It is true that this is a life-long process, but you will be winning ground your entire life. That sounds good to me, how about you?

Step 1

Decide. Choose. Plan. You have to shoot at a target. Generalized positive and biblical thinking is good; but if you want to renew, which indicates that there is something inside of you that needs to have a makeover, you have to target it. As Brian Tracy would say, "You have to find the biggest frog in the pond and eat it."[9] When I first did this, it was rejection. I listed everything that rejection did to me, all the thoughts associated with it, and all the belief systems that it birthed in me. That was my target. What was its antithesis? Acceptance. Fortunate for me God accepts me, but that didn't make it easy, it just made it doable. Pick a target. What do you want to replace in your thinking? What is going to replace it?

Step 2

Think. Ponder. Meditate. Now you concentrate on the replacement thought. You don't concentrate on not thinking the negative, ungodly or harmful thought. If you think about not thinking about it, you *are* thinking about it. This is why the, "don't do..." solutions don't work. You spend your time thinking about what you are not supposed to do, which means that your mind is occupied with the very thing you are trying not to do. If you are dealing with anger and hostility, you replace it with grace, mercy, love, peace or whatever else would be helpful for you. You have to think deeply about what you want to build in your brain.

Christian meditation has been lost. I think we are afraid to

99

meditate because of the eastern type of meditation where they think about nothing or their navel, which is incongruent with Christian beliefs. So we have thrown out God's Word with our avoidance of any New Age leanings. Meditation is talked about in the Bible, mostly in the Psalms. Meditation and heart have a connection in scripture and they do in our lives as well. As much as our mind and brains need renewing, so does our brain in our heart. That's right. I said *brain in our heart*. We actually have one. Some claim we have a brain in our gut too. "My gut feeling is…," or "My heart is telling me…," or "What I think is…" All of these mindsets need renewing. They are connected like every part of us is connected.

To meditate is to think about, to chew on, to roll over in one's mind. Meditation is not memorization. Meditation gets it deep. You not only think about what it means, dissecting the thought or verse(s) to understand them, but you put yourself in the thought or in the verse. Let's take Philippians 4:13 as an example.

> *I can do everything through him who gives me strength.*
> (Philippians 4:13)

When meditating on this verse, you take 5-10 minutes and think about it from every angle. This is not some kind of dreamy, eastern, wishful New Age thinking; this is forecasting the Word of God to be true in your life.

I can do. Think about what you can do. Not it happening to you, but you actually doing it.

Everything. There isn't anything that you can't do. You don't like public speaking, but you can do it. See yourself successfully giving the speech. How are you going to be able to speak publically, or whatever it is that you can do?

Through God. What does that mean? How does that look? How does that operate?

Who gives me strength. His strength is going to work in you and through you. God gives you the strength. What do you look like with God's strength? How is life different? How do you think and behave with God's strength working through you and in you? Use your God given imagination. Play a movie in your head. Have a conversation with yourself.

Step 3

Arrest. Jail. Execute. When opposing thoughts come into your head, you have to detain them, and if need be, kill them. The battlefield for this fight you are in is located between your ears and in your mind. Passivity is our death angel. Passivity in our thinking is like letting someone burn you with a smoldering match over and over again until he ran out of matches. One touch and a healthy person would tell that person to stop and enforce that command. We cannot afford to let opposing thoughts to camp in our heads. We have to arrest them immediately and kick them out.

When I was at the brain seminar by Dr. Leaf, I remember her talking about the person whose mind is going all the time. From the time they wake up until the time they go to bed, their mind is thinking non-stop about 20 different things. I thought, "That is me." Her solution on how to stop that from happening didn't make me happy, but it was true. It was, *control your thinking.* Well, duh! How do you do that? Discipline. Just like I discipline myself in my eating, I have to discipline myself in my thinking. Maybe you are thinking, "I am not very disciplined." That is a problem—with most of us. Here is the good news: you can change! Maybe that is your first identified thought you go after, "I am not disciplined." Remember, you "can do all things through Christ who strengthens you" (Philippians 4:13 NKJV). So set your mind to it and make up your mind right now. You will identify every thought that comes into your mind and you will make sure it lines up with God.

> We demolish arguments and every pretension that sets itself up against the knowledge of God, and we take captive every thought to make it obedient to Christ. (2 Corinthians 10:5)

God is with you. All His resources are behind you. He has committed Himself to your success in this and every other thing in His Word. You can do it!

Step 4

Write. Journal. Record. I have never liked to journal. I don't write that neat. However, I do type fast. So with my iPad and with what I felt was an urge from God, I began journaling a few years ago. What I found is that writing was cathartic for me. I would begin to write and through that process my thinking would open up and things that I had not thought about—different views of things, different applications of truth—would begin to emerge from me. It was as if writing activated a different side of my brain. In a sense, it did. Writing involves more of you. Not only is it a wonderful output, but because you are looking at it with your eyes, it involves input as well. You can read what you wrote, what God spoke to you, and your observations of your thoughts or behaviors. When you look back at what you have written you will see patterns that you have never seen before. You see things differently, which starts another process—review. The power of keeping a journal or record cannot be overstated. If you were like me, and basically hated the thought of it, try it for six months; or if that was overwhelming, try it for one month. We write differently than we talk. My observation is that it helps clarify things and illuminates your heart.

Step 5

Say. Speak. Preach. Speaking things out loud is so powerful. It is how God created the world. He didn't think, "Let there be light." He said it. Proverbs tells us that we are ensnared by the words we speak. Words are full of power.

> *The tongue has the power of life and death, and those who love it will eat its fruit.* (Proverbs 18:21)

Life and death, positive and negative, blessing and cursing all can come from your mouth. This last step cannot be skipped. It is powerful for many reasons, not the least of which is you hear yourself speak. There is this circuit that happens when we speak. It is more than just we think, we speak, we hear, we think, but speaking and hearing engages the heart. You can randomly and mindlessly repeat things; I understand that. However, when you are thinking something that you know to be true and you are speaking it, your heart engages because your heart is actually engaged in discerning truth. Jesus said, "For out of the abundance of the heart, the mouth speaks" (Luke 6:45 NKJV). This means that you need to be listening to yourself. Making sure that your mouth and mind are lined up with want you want to be like.

You can undo what you have been thinking by speaking things that are antagonistic to your new or renewing thoughts. Didn't our mom's tell us, "If you can't say something nice, don't say anything at all?" I ditto that. How many times has our mouth gotten us into trouble? The beauty is that your mouth can get you out of trouble too. Start preaching to yourself. Look in the mirror and say, "I am beautiful" (or handsome), or "I am smart," or "I am well able to get this done." In fact, putting the Word of God on your tongue wouldn't hurt either. Confession means saying the same thing. So start saying the same thing that God says. You will find yourself being lifted up and changing.

How Much?

You have this little thing inside your brain called the amygdala and one of its jobs it to be your safety officer. It doesn't like to change. It likes to keep things the same. To override this impulse you have to be purposeful, consistent and have the desire to follow through. Remember, this is a 21-day process and I would recommend that you work steps 2-5 at least every day. At the end of the process the "biggies" may not be completely done. They have been engrained for quite some time and it will take longer than 21 days to get rid of all the negative thought connections to your life. My comment to that is—so what? Life is waiting for you. Getting rid of the thoughts of rejection, stupidity, ugliness, and failure are possible. The thoughts of acceptance, intelligence, beauty, success and the like are waiting. Those negative thoughts may linger, but they won't be predominate trees in the forest of my mind. They will be seeds that try to germinate and I will kick them out as many times as I have to. You will too. The effort is worth it. Winning is exhilarating. Everyone connected to you will be happy about it if they are healthy. God will be glorified.

8

Emotional Part of the Whole

This is an area of such hope and such possibility and even probable progress! So many, including myself, have been victim to our own emotions. Yet there is so much hope for change. It is within our grasp. First, we have to see the need for at least a tune up if not a complete overhaul. Are you ready for change? Admittedly this is my area of trouble, an area of great interest to me personally. Judging from the overwhelming statistics regarding burnout and stress disease and all that comes with it, I am not the only one. I am continually ready for more freedom and elevation in this area of life, and I know you are too.

There are all kinds of dangerous and deadly emotions. There are also many wonderful emotions that bring about positive changes, some of which create a healthy flow throughout our body and brain. We get to choose which ones win the war within us. All of us would choose love over indifference or hate, and we would choose peace over turmoil and upheaval. Likewise, we would choose faith over fear, and forgiveness over hostility, right? Do we? Think about it for a moment. I know you would want to, but do you? All of these negative emotions stress us out. They produce a stress response within our bodies that does harm and not good. In addition to the above-mentioned negative emotions there are plenty more that wreak havoc in your body.

For some the struggle isn't hate or bitterness, it is life's pressing machine. It is being under the constant weight of life and having it continue to barrage you with artillery. It is the unrelenting attack of daily living with all of its stress and strain that gets us. When deadlines are pressing, what happens inside? When disappointment happens or interpersonal fights take place, what happens inside? Stress. If continually carried these stressors will cause harmful, long-term effects to many or all of our six areas. That is a big problem.

The body's natural response to stress should last only seconds to a couple of minutes. It is meant to be a burst. You have heard of the flight or fight response, haven't you? (I actually think there should be a third type, which is "freeze"—like a deer in headlights). This response comes as a survival mechanism endowed to us by our Creator. Have you ever seen a cheetah hunting a gazelle? The cheetah sneaks up on a pack of gazelles and as soon as any of the gazelles sensed or heard the cheetah's presence, guess what happened? A stress response. They would freeze and the cheetah would see that he has been discovered and charge the easiest prey. The gazelle would run like crazy to get away. Both animals are in full stress response. Their adrenals are pumping to help them. For the cheetah, he has got to eat so he needs to catch the gazelle. For the gazelle, he is trying to survive. The cheetah can hit forty-five MPH within four strides; the gazelle doesn't have a chance, right? The gazelle is equipped with good cornering and he tries to out maneuver the cheetah. If you have ever watched a chase in which the gazelle out corners the cheetah, how long is the chase? Usually under a minute. This high burst of energy aided by a stress response isn't supposed to last long. Either the cheetah stays hungry or catches its feast, but the chase will be over within a minute.

We may not be a cheetah or gazelle, but our stress response is meant for the same reason. It is to help us get out of danger or overcome the danger. Stress response helps us focus mentally and physically, but it is meant to be for a short time. Then we are supposed to rest and let our body return to a normal state. The problem with being under stress all the time, whether you actually need the stress response or not and whether it is good stress (winning a car on The Price is Right) or bad stress, our body's response needs to be for a short term.

Did I say good stress? Yes. There is good stress. Exhilaration is good stress. I have gone skydiving and believe me when I say that there is a massive stress response when you jump out of an airplane at 12,000 feet. It is the same as when you ride on a roller coaster. Stress happens. Again, that is not a bad thing unless it is overused. There are adrenaline junkies like there are alcoholics and heroin addicts. They thrive on adrenaline. They are looking for the next high. They love being risky. They create situations that will stimulate their brains to send the signal to the pituitary gland to signal the adrenals to secret the good stuff. They are seriously addicted to the good stuff. When there is no physical challenge or danger that they can put themselves into, they create it in their minds. They fantasize about different scenarios that will give them an adrenal response. Some of you who just like to relax are saying, really? Yes, really.

Before we criticize the adrenaline junkies of this world who create the opportunity for a stress response, we better take a look within ourselves and gain some understanding of our own addictions. Most people fall into three different categories when it comes to stress. The first category is the people who have it whipped. They are fully engaged in life and have learned how to manage the stresses of life without overstressing their bodies, brains and relationships. The second category is the above mentioned adrenaline addict. Before you dismiss yourself from that category, think about the turmoil in your life. Some people feel more comfortable with some kind of turmoil or deadline. It may not be jumping a motorcycle 90 feet that excites you; rather it may be conflict, deadlines, perfect performances and the like. If you like inserting yourself into drama and stir your own pot often, you may be an adrenaline junkie yourself. The third category is where most of us rest. Rest wasn't the right word. In fact we don't rest. We go, and go, and go, and go, and when we are done going we go some more. There are hundreds of things to do and we have got to do them. We have work to do, money to make, casseroles to bake, kids to take, dogs to walk, trees to lop and groceries to shop. Our lives are so full that when we have an evening at home with nothing to do we get amazed.

Most people can't get going in the morning without a cup of coffee (or a few cups of coffee) and some can't slow down at the end of the day without a glass of wine or other alcohol. (I know I just stepped on the sacred cow of the west: coffee. I am not saying you have to give it up, I am just pointing out that if you need it to get your engine going because your engine needs a boost, your engine may be over performing). For others it is playing Internet games of fighting and war, or watching thrilling things on TV. Did you know that when you play those games or you watch a show or movie with life threatening situations it triggers a stress response in you? It is nearly the same as being there in a real life situation.

So what? That's what some will say. *So what if I am going all the time, or do thrilling things or like to watch high-energy movies and TV. I'm fine.* Others will know that they have to slow down and change. I am imploring all of us to change. Our overstressing is causing great damage to our systems. Stress response, as I define it, is how we internally handle external and internal stressors. How you deal with life is your stress response. Remember, stress isn't bad in the short-term. It is harmful when it is a long-term happening (a happening is described in the chapter Torpedoes That Can Sink You). When the chemicals cortisol, norepinephrine and epinephrine are flowing through your blood stream in high levels constantly, that is what creates all kinds of havoc.

Negative, harmful, dangerous and deadly emotions like unforgiveness, bitterness, resentment, hatred, hostility, fear and so on, create a stress response in your body. They essentially make you stressed out. Let's look at what happens to our bodies when we are stressed and overstressed (the state of constant stress).

When you are stressed, your blood pressure goes up and your heart rate increases. Your digestion shuts down as blood is sent to the muscles that will need to run from danger or fight through the danger. The cardiovascular problem arises from too much triglycerides (fats) running through your blood stream all the time. High amounts of blood sugar and insulin are released into the blood system from your body thinking it needs energy to survive. Your thyroid gets involved to regulate energy usage and, therefore, in a state of overstress it is being overused, as are the adrenals. (Both are controlled by the pituitary gland.) Your body then produces more cholesterol just in case it needs it and all have a deadly result over time.

Too much stress enlarges the adrenal glands by the over-stimulated pituitary gland. (The pituitary signals the release of stress hormones.) The problem here is there are too many hormones flowing through the body and it creates a hormonal imbalance. We are used to seeing this in some women during their menstrual cycle. Overstressing creates imbalances that affect mood, thinking, impulse control, weight retention and other things.

Cortisol—a stress hormone—over time will keep your blood sugar and insulin levels high and causes you to retain mid-section fat. (That is where the body stores fat that it will need for quick energy.) It depletes bones of vital calcium, magnesium and potassium and retains salt. It impairs immune function and response, reduces muscle mass, inhibits skin growth and regeneration, and impairs memory and learning. Other damaging effects of cortisol include a decrease in bone formation and collagen loss in the skin.[1] That translates to wrinkles. (Now I have the attention of every woman.)

I did a lot of research on the effects of cortisol on our bodies while writing this book. The facts are everywhere, yet we still need to get a deeper understanding of them. I don't think most of us really understand what stress is doing to our bodies. The above-mentioned effects are just scratching the surface. I have included a little more research to help dig deeper into these issues.

- One effect of the stress response is to break down adipose (fat) cells to move triglycerides (fat molecules) into the bloodstream for more energy. Your body uses the energy from triglycerides in the "fight or flight" physical response to stress. But do you have increased physical activity in response to most of the stresses you experience in the modern world? Most people don't. Instead of burning the triglycerides, cortisol causes these unused fats to be re-deposited in the adipose tissues surrounding the belly.[2]

- The body stores unused stress energy around the abdominal organs. Accumulation of this specific type of fat is known as visceral fat and is most damaging to our health, leading to an increased development of cardiovascular disease, high blood pressure and diabetes. The problem is we often deal with stress mentally, and never respond to stress with physical activity that would burn the extra energy provided by the cortisol surge. Whether your stress was emotional or physical, the stress response is identical, causing a spike in your appetite. This can cause a craving for comfort foods—foods high in fat and sugar.[3]

- Elevated cortisol levels from prolonged or chronic stress can cause side effects such as suppression of thyroid function, cognitive impairment, increased blood pressure, decreased bone density, and blood sugar imbalances. High levels of cortisol can also lower your immunity and inflammatory responses, as well as slow down the wound healing process.[4]
- Chronic high concentration of cortisol is toxic to brain cells and can cause short-term memory loss. A lifetime of high cortisol levels may be a primary contributor to Alzheimer's disease and senile dementia. High cortisol is also a primary cause of osteoporosis.[5]
- Cortisol suppresses the immune system by "muting" the white blood cells.[6]
- When your body faces toxic thoughts and emotions, it cannot discern its true enemy and attacks healthy cells and tissue, losing its ability to fight the true invaders.[7]
- It shuts down the reproductive system, resulting in an increased chance of miscarriage and (in some cases) temporary infertility. Fertility returns after cortisol levels return to normal.[8]

Stress triggers many negative reactions including heart issues such as heart palpitations, chest pain, and it affects the joints, the muscles, the lungs, the bowels, the brain, your sleep, your sex life and gives you a headache. Overstressing pretty much ruins your life, ages you quicker and even ruins your relationships.

Do I have your attention yet? Stress isn't okay. It is not a badge of honor or importance. We need to get that into our core belief system and remove it from our lives.

All of the deadly emotions like hatred, bitterness and fear trigger a stress response in the body and that includes the brain. When those emotions are running through your body it is like putting your body and brain under stress and never letting it rest. There are certain emotions that are well studied with their effects on health. Let me name a few:

Hostility – If you are a hostile person who is ready to blow at any moment, you are 3-5 times more likely to die of cardiovascular disease and 7 times less likely to live past fifty. It may be a better predictor than smoking for high blood pressure.[9]

Fear – "Research shows that fear triggers more than 1,400 known physical and chemical responses. This activates more than 30 different hormones and neurotransmitters combined, throwing the body into a frantic state."[10]

The reason you can't get away with negative emotions without it affecting your body is that you have a wonderful communication system between your brain and your immune system. The brain produces neuropeptides, which communicate with a certain class of immune cells called monocytes. They communicate back and forth to one another and more than that, these immune cells and other cells have memory. They remember what the communications were and especially the incessant communication of something that happens a lot. It can be negative, but the good news is that it also can be positive. You have a choice in the matter of stress. You may not be able to control the outside forces upon you or the external pressures to a great extent, but you can control what goes on inside of you. You can control how you process and what you do with what is going on in your life and in your mind. As I have said before, the mind is where this battle will be won or lost. How you process the world around you, the information coming to you, and how you fit into your surroundings is determined by your thinking. How you think determines how you react. You are nobody's victim.

As I explained in the previous chapter, your thoughts are physical structures in your brain. Emotions are chemicals that are attached to thoughts. You cannot deny the presence of an emotional response but you can determine how that response will play out. Let's say you were really hurt by somebody in your family. When you see them again, or when that instance is brought up, your memory (thought structure) comes to your cognitive mind and with it the emotion that is attached to it. The only way to stop that from happening is to renew the mind with a different thought structure. When the emotional response comes it can even trigger a physiological response. These emotions are *real*. You don't overcome them by telling yourself that they are not there. Buried emotions will have a resurrection day at the worst possible time or at a disconnected happening. You have got to experience the emotion and deal with it. It is *how* you deal with it that is key. You have control over how you deal with it. If you let that emotion have its way, it will roll around in your head for hours, days or even longer—years. You can control your emotional expression and you can control how long you get to think about it.

I am going to get to the how-to in a couple of pages, but let me give you an example in my life. As a small church pastor for many years, I was devastated when someone left the church. The hurt and betrayal that I felt when people left because I wasn't good enough was difficult to get past. I care deeply—too deeply at times—about how people view me, and as a small church anyone leaving was an earthquake with visible results. The only thing that could circumvent my going over and over it in my mind with gushing negative emotions was to pray for the person or family who left, every time that I thought of them or the circumstance. It didn't stop me from feeling the emotion, but it did stop me from being its victim. I prayed for their lives to go well and for God to bless them. It turned me around and stopped the negative thought cycle as well as the stress response produced by the hurt in the now and the fear of the future.

Before we go any further, let's have a humorous look at stress. I don't know about you, but if I can laugh about it, I can deal with it better. This is not to say that you should just laugh off your overstressed life, but sometimes you just have to lighten up a little bit. Indulge me for a minute.

Top 10 ways to be stressed out:

1. Don't say no to anything! Get overloaded and stay there.
2. Don't plan at all, just flow.
3. Wait until the last minute to do anything—and hurry!
4. Receive anything said to you that isn't 100% loving as an offense.
5. Obsess on everything—just keep thinking about all the bad stuff over and over.
6. Always want more; never be satisfied.
7. Expect perfection out of everyone, especially yourself.
8. Don't relax, just keep going; you can rest in heaven.

9. Let everything frustrate you.
10. Worry about everything.
11. Don't eat well, sleep enough, rest enough, enjoy life enough and certainly don't exercise or take time for yourself!
12. Think about how stressed out everything makes you—all the time!
13. Be afraid—of everything. Especially things that have very little chance of happening.
14. Talk about how stressed out you are and keep talking about all the things that are going wrong in your life.
(I was too stressed out to narrow it down to 10.)

So you were laughing, but you saw yourself in there, didn't you? Maybe you just cracked a grin as you thought about what you were reading. We are all in there to one extent or the other. Take a deep breath and keep reading.

Cool things you get from staying stressed out:

1. Fat. Belly fat is cortisol's specialty—getting fat without eating a ton!
2. Heart disease, hypertension, and jagged vessel walls, which is a precursor to arteriosclerosis—a quicker ride to heaven
3. Type 2 diabetes. Stress causes your cells to be insulin resistant. Say good-bye to Slurpees and hello to insulin shots daily.
4. ED in men and PMS and other menstruation problems in women. Hey, it's free birth control.
5. Memory loss. It messes with the hippocampus and messes with cells' ability of glucose uptake. At least you won't remember why you're stressed out.
6. Depression. People will feel sorry for you and maybe you will get more gifts.
7. Bone loss. Stress causes bone cell production to slow. If you were too tall, maybe you will shrink and get in and out of the car easier.
8. Decreased immune function. You get to be sick more—or rather catch up on your TV shows and read all the free magazines at your doctor's office.

9. Autoimmune disease. This is your body attacking your body. I can't think of anything fun about this. (This is most likely tied into toxic emotions and other things.)
10. You get to know your doctor as well as his golfing buddies.
11. Complete mental/emotional/physical breakdown. You won't have to work anymore!

I could go on and on but hopefully I have convinced you to take a serious look at your stress levels and how you live. Seventy-five percent of all doctor visits and hospitalizations are stress related. Let's tackle this thing before it tackles us. It is easier than you think.

As I said before, it all starts with how you process the world around you, the information coming to you, and how you fit into your surroundings. It starts with how we think, which is under our direct control. The first thing we all must do is figure out what stresses us out and why. Some people are so unaware of their present condition. They live on autopilot. If that is you, take yourself off autopilot and begin to fly the plane. You will need to feel all the bumps, see the horizon and read all the gauges from here on out. Answer these questions when you are stressed out. I encourage you to go through these questions at the end of every day. You will learn a lot about yourself and what triggers prolonged stress response.

- What causes me to start feeling stressed?
- From what activity or when did I first start feeling stressed?
- What was my thinking that allowed me to overstress?
- What is the root belief that allowed for or caused that thinking?

If you answer those questions honestly and with insight, you launch out of the starting blocks on your quest to live without being stressed out. The first step is to get a handle on your triggers. What gets you?

I have figured out my number one stressor. It took a while but after carefully assessing my life time and time again, I figured it out. It's time. Every day seemed to stress me out if I didn't get it all done, and I rarely got it all done except when I was on vacation. When I was on vacation it took me three to five days to relax and let myself completely enjoy it without having to do something. Maybe instead of naming it time, it is really productivity, or more accurately an unreasonable expectation to produce.

If your schedule controls you, you will be its servant. If you control your schedule, it will serve you. I like serving and all, but I think I want to be the master in this scenario. (I will discuss more about mastering your schedule in the Planning Your Life chapter.) At the end of every day I was stressed out as well as during the day because I saw that I wasn't going to get it all done. What do you choose not to do? What I learned was that I couldn't choose in the middle of the day, I had to choose at the beginning of the day or better yet, at the beginning of the week. When you schedule your week or even your day, you see that you can't possibly get it all done and you have to choose. When I do that, I am relieved of undue stress and I can think better and produce more throughout my day.

After understanding our triggers, it may even lead to a life adjustment or as I call it, an elevation to the next level of living. The above example was like that. There was a core belief that I needed to address in order to make the initial change happen. So how about that core belief?

There is a core belief that allows us to stress out. Either we need to be in control or it is tapping into our belief of inadequacy or some other core belief that enables a continued adrenal response of a prolonged and deadly nature. In my case, it was the fantastic performance syndrome. (That is not a known psychological disorder, but it should be.) I wanted to be a fantastic performer so much so that I wanted to be able to get it all done and done well. There is nothing wrong with that thinking except when it defines you as a person. When I didn't get it all done, I felt bad about my performance. Even though I got a lot done, it was never good enough. And when I didn't get everything done that I thought should be done, it created a lack of value in me. That lack of value pressed me to perform better and produce more, which stressed me out. Perfectionism? Yes it was, but I can now allow myself to be imperfect. If you read my rough draft of this book you would know what I speak is truth.

Are you seeing it? My surface stressor was time, but my core belief was about performance. What about you? Think about the last time you were stressed out and go back and answer those questions. See what you come up with about your own stressors. After you get a handle on what you respond to and how you respond to it, you can dig deeper to determine the why. Why do you feel stress? Armed with your why, you are now ready to take on the dragon and win peace and good health.

Slaying the Dragon of Stress

Can you guess where we are going to start? Your thought life. How you interpret the exterior and interior stressors can be the only starting place. If you know the root belief that keeps stress hanging around too long, you have to get rid of that belief. It is like that *friend* that comes over and never leaves. They eat your food, they take up the whole couch while watching TV, they leave a mess everywhere and they don't do any chores. It is time to kick them out. How? You have to replace the wrong thinking with right thinking—healthy, life-giving thinking.

Begin to meditate on correct thinking. Apply scripture to your life. Meditate on it and see it working out in your future. God has given us a wonderful gift of imagination. Use it. This is so much more than wishful thinking; this is replacing your thinking. You have to fill your mind with the right stuff.

Once you have done this once, do it again and again. In fact, do it for several months—three is a nice number. You will understand yourself. You will understand your thinking that is deadly. You will come up with a strategy because you really are quite a smart person. It takes effort and it takes courage as well as some longsuffering. There is no overnight miracle except if God grants you one. In cases like this, He usually wants you to work it out so change comes and you are more like His original design. Ask those four questions above at the end of every day at a minimum. Then renew your mind. You know how to do that.

> You will keep in perfect peace all who trust in you, all whose thoughts are fixed on you! (Isaiah 26:3 NLT)

There is nothing like trusting God with your situation, circumstance, and entire life to bring peace where there was stress.

See yourself in this verse. What does it look like to trust in God in your present situation? What is it like to have all your thoughts fixed on God? What would you be doing if that were reality? What does perfect peace look like? See yourself in perfect peace. Feel yourself in perfect peace. Slow down and picture it. I have an Arnold Palmer sitting on a warm beachscape. How about you? You don't have to imagine going there in times of turmoil, you have to capture what it is like to be there and bring that into your present. This isn't easy, but it is so wonderful when you have mastered it. God wants you to stay there, in perfect peace. There is no stress there. It's like nothing is nipping at your heals or trying to devour you, right? Living a life like that is possible, but it is going to take a change in the way you operate. It is going to take honesty, strength, effort and resource. You can do it. It is yours to attain.

By the way, as an interesting side note, perfect peace in the Hebrew is, "Shalom, shalom." It's like one peace wasn't enough. Shalom is so much more than peace. It is completeness and soundness. Now go back and read those words again. Nice, huh?

Measures to Reduce Stress

So far, we've discussed some deeper ways to reduce stress: 1) go through the questions a few pages back and getting real with yourself about stress; and 2) renew your mind to change the way you think about yourself, your surroundings and your stressors. But there are also a number of ways to make some quick improvements.

<u>Dump It</u>

The first one comes from a book I just read by my friend Ralph Moore called *Stress Busters*. (It is a good book.) He talks about emptying your mind of the clutter and staying focused on one thing at a time instead of having dozens of thoughts rolling around in your brain.[11] I don't remember if he taught me years ago about this, but I have applied this principle when I read my Bible because I want to concentrate on what I am reading and I usually read in the morning when my mind is spinning fast. I write down all the "gotta do's" that came to mind on a piece of paper and tend to them later so I can concentrate on the Word. Ralph takes this further and applies this principle to your whole life and throughout your whole day. Whenever you have extra thoughts rolling around, things you have to do or things you want to do or just things, drop them in a to do list. He uses Toodledo, I use Producteev, and there are probably 100 other free apps that will sync your lists with all of your devices. That is what you want— something that can quickly record your thoughts so you can let them go and retrieve them on your smartphone, iPad, laptop, PC or MAC (or your microwave, if it has that capability). The point here, as Ralph puts it, is to "dump" the extra thoughts so you can concentrate on one at a time.

Schedule It

It is amazing how calendaring things can give you peace because you know you have time to get them done. Plus the added bonus of filling out a calendar hour by hour is that you see that you can't get it all done that day so you don't expect to get it done. What a relief. In addition to that, you can schedule days off, vacations, date nights, game night with the kids and all kinds of things that get crowded out if you have a busy schedule. One piece of advice, do not make an appointment without looking at your calendar. You may double book yourself because you dumped the thought of doing that thing that you put on your calendar a week ago. Always check your calendar before saying yes to more.

Time Out

You need a daily time out. Remember kindergarten? Oh, how I long for naptime in the afternoon. So take one! You will be 20-30% more productive in the second half of the day if you take a short nap. Some companies are installing nap rooms. Why? They want to increase productivity. For you I would suggest that this time is just rest without a thought of all the other benefits. If you can't take a short nap, then take a three-minute vacation. Just breathe and relax and think about God. Shalom, shalom.

Exercise

We discussed all the great benefits of exercise in the Physical Part of the Whole chapter, but it has to be mentioned again here. Exercise releases all kinds of wonderful things including feel good messengers that travel throughout your body telling other cells that things are good. Exercise actually reduces cortisol levels. So when you are stressed out, go for a run and you will be less stressed when you return. (Unless you're not a runner, then you may be stressed out because your knees hurt.) Whatever you have to do, get moving and enjoy it. The enjoyment of activity will compound the wonderful effect on your body and the reduction of cortisol.

Eating Habits

Feeding our body the right things is paramount to its homeostasis (balance). When we eat garbage we retain the garbage and our body can only do so well with garbage. If you eat healthier, you will be healthier and that means your ability to think will be healthier. Don't be misguided into thinking that you can eat whatever you want and still think the same. That is a lie. In order for your neurotransmitters to work effectively, everything has to be in balance. Eating a bunch of sugary items will throw your brain chemistry off in seconds. Also, laying off the caffeine and all of those energy drinks would help a great deal as well. Your body isn't made to be overstimulated with all those substances that act like amphetamines in your system. I am not saying never drink any of them, I am simply saying that cutting back and watching when you drink them would reduce your stress level.

Supplements

There are several great stress busting supplements you can take, and I'll name two of them here. The first is Omega 3 fatty acids. This will benefit you far beyond your stress levels, but it will reduce you cortisol levels. The second is Vitamin C. How easy. Take some pills and reduce your stress. Just remember, it won't eradicate your stress, it just helps to reduce it.

Sleep

Recovery is essential for your body and for your brain, and sleep is the only thing that will provide this recovery. Shoot for 7.5 hours per night, which is 5 sleep cycles. (The amount of sleep one needs is contested, but 7.5 hours is a fair assumption). If you can do more, go for 9 hours. However, research is showing that anything above that could be detrimental to your health.

Sunlight

We need sunlight. There is a disorder that hits many people in the US called seasonal affective disorder. You can boil it down to this: people are depressed because they don't get sunlight on their skin. We need to get out in the sun. Easy for me to say living in Southern California, but this is no joke. Sunlight reduces your stress levels.

Touch

Everyone needs touch. Touch actually reduces cortisol levels in the blood stream. So everyone go out and get a massage. (Masseuses may thank me for that plug with a free massage.) We are becoming a touch unwanted nation. For all kinds of reasons people touch less. We aren't comfortable with it. So for some, touch will stress them out, which is so sad. The very thing that brings benefit instead brings stress. Sex is touch and it goes way beyond touch to reduce stress. A warning to husbands: When you have had an argument with your wife, assuming things got worked out, an hour later your cortisol levels are near normal, while you wife's won't be normal for hours (up to eight). So when you suggest going together to your room and she wants nothing to do with that, give her a massage. (Ladies, you're welcome.)

Laughing

Laughing is great medicine and brings all kinds of health benefits. Laughing, and crying by the way, reduces cortisol levels. So put on America's Funniest Videos and de-stress. There are many more things, but that should get you started on your way to stress-free living.

All of these things along with the four questions to evaluate yourself need to be constantly reviewed in your life. If you are like me, you will implement these things because you are at some kind of crises or near a crisis. After the crisis has been averted, you will go back to your typical stressed out, Type A or whatever you want to call it, life. This is a life-long thing. There are people who you would never know are stressed out until they have strokes, heart disease or Alzheimer's, and there are people that are obviously stressed out. Wouldn't it be nice to have some friends or loved ones that would tell you if they see you going down a bad path? Oh, that would be a scary thought, right? *Nobody is going to evaluate me and be my life coach!* Well, if you are stressed out and it just isn't a season of stress, like living through a hurricane or losing your job, then you better listen up to the above advice. If you are like me you are bothered very little from dropping dead of a heart attack. It would be bad for my family, but I will be in heaven. However, a stroke…a debilitating stroke, that would be bad! Not being able to do things for yourself, like eating, dressing or going to the bathroom—that would be hell, or at least purgatory! You now are loaded with some knowledge about stress, and if you want more there is tons of it out there.

Why roll the dice with life? Master stress and enjoy life. Don't wait any longer. This dragon needs to be slain—over and over again. You are equipped to do it. You have some knowledge now and you have the aptitude endowed to you by your Creator. Ask Him for help. He wants you to be in peace.

> *Peace I leave with you; my peace I give you. I do not give to you as the world gives. Do not let your hearts be troubled and do not be afraid.* (John 14:27)

> *I have told you these things, so that in me you may have peace. In this world you will have trouble. But take heart! I have overcome the world.* (John 16:33)

9

Relational Part of the Whole

There is a beautiful Hebrew legend of two brothers who lived side by side on adjoining lands. One was the head of a large family, the other lived alone. One night, the former lay awake and thought: "My brother lives alone, he has not the companionship of wife and children to cheer his heart as I have. While he sleeps, I will carry some of my sheaves into his field."

At the same hour, the other brother reasoned: "My brother has a large family, and his necessities are greater than mine. As he sleeps, I will put some of my sheaves on his side of the field." Thus the two brothers went out, each carrying out his purposes and each laden with sheaves—and met at the dividing line. There they embraced. [1]

We are meant to be connected. Doesn't that resonate true? Think about the hermits you would see on "Gunsmoke" (wow, dating myself again). I am talking about those people who lived in the mountains and didn't come in contact with people except for the scene you were watching. Didn't you feel sorry for them or at least think to yourself, "That would be weird." (I know that mothers of large families might be tempted to desire that life, but trust me, you would hate it—after two weeks). Yes, it would be weird and actually it would be unhealthy! We need connection and more than that, some human touch would be great too!

From the beginning of time we were made to love; to give love and to receive love from the heart, selflessly, extravagantly and lavishly. If we are connected to the inner parts of us that are untainted or that have been regenerated, we will know the sense of pleasure that comes from loving deeply. The love between a man and woman is cataclysmic. It takes over the world around us. When you have it, you could forget everything and just live for it, but it wasn't meant for that. It has brought down mighty men and women when it was unchecked and it has augmented forever the path that some were on. It does change you; you are different after that kind of love. It is meant to do that. It is meant to bring us into a greater destiny and a more extraordinary purpose.

Friendships that are forged and bonded are like soldiers or Marines and others who would risk their own life to save their comrade. We are meant to have friendships that are close. We are created with the desire to help our buddy, to have a meaningful place in the life of another. We may not be glad for the 2:00 a.m. call that they are broken down on the side of the road, nor may we be happy about our decision to go get them or fix their car, but when we are there for a friend, satisfaction rises up in us. It is significance.

Yet, there has been a taming of this creator-deposited desire. Selfishness has risen and we have decided to guard our hearts with barbwire and let nobody passed the fortress wall into our inner sanctum—our heart, our core. Even though this hasn't worked out very well for us, or for society, we keep doing it. Maybe we partitioned some of our heart so we won't give it all away. Whatever the case, we need to come back to reality. We need to come back to our design. We were created to love, be loved and be a part of something bigger than ourselves.

Studies on DNA have confirmed this predisposition to love and to be loved. In a study at the Institute of HeartMath, researchers found that negative emotions, produced at will by the research subjects, caused the two strands that comprise human DNA to wind more tightly. On the other hand, heart-centered feelings of love and appreciation caused the DNA strands to unwind and exhibit positive changes in just two minutes.[2,3] How incredible is that! Heartfelt love changes your DNA in a positive manner, which brings positive results to your entire being. We were wired for heartfelt love.

Could it be that love is some type of energy? I know it is a motivator. You will do things when you love deeply that you would never do when that love is absent. Could it be that within the body and the brain that love produces an energy that brings all kinds of benefits? I think so; just another wonderful gift from our Creator. We have been told the benefits for millennia, and now science has confirmed it. Love produces good stuff. Hatred, bitterness and the like produce bad stuff. Love brings health. Bitterness brings disease.

Can't you see bitterness on people's faces? The older they get the more you can see it. It changes the shape of their face. They look angry. They have a certain presence about them; the kind that makes you to not want to be around them. It comes out in their speech whether or not they are talking about something or someone that they have bitterness towards. It seems to leak from the fiber of their being. Now you know why. They have changed their DNA, sometimes for decades. Are you attracted to them? If you are, you are in trouble.

Love attracts. Isaac Newton watched the apple fall from the tree and told others that the apple was attracted to the earth. Poetry has made much of the attraction of the moon to the earth in the context of love. In fact, there are electromagnetic waves that are produced by love that attract others to you. People have written many books about the "law of attraction." I don't know what they have said, but let me save you some money. Love others, and you will be more attractive.

So how about those guys who are basically jerks yet always get the pretty girls? What gives? Brokenness. It is like a woman being drawn to an abuser. It is love defiled; love that isn't really love. It's gone wrong, terribly wrong. It is like the fact that when I said the word *love*, some automatically thought sex. We should know the difference, especially in this day when sex is so cheap. "Friends with benefits" is a phrase used for people who have no romantic love between them but engage in sex. Empty. Deformed. Such a waste; such a cheap substitute. I honestly feel for people with this ill thinking; those who think some physical act of eroticism is love or has nothing to do with love, as well as those who are attracted to jerks, controllers and/or unhealthy relationships. It is the quest for love gone wrong. It's truly sad. God wants to bring us back to real love.

We all want real love. Whether familial, friendship or romantic, we want it. We search for it. We often define ourselves by it. Our quest for love is never ending. We want to be loved and we want to love. That is who we are. I think that is why some settle for broken love. At least it is love of some sort. Don't settle. There are real friends and a real love that is waiting in God's wings. Sometimes, most of the time, we have to let go of the broken branch to grab onto the healthy one. You can do it.

The Benefits of Community

I think much of this research about relationships (as well as research about health after retirement) shows that we need purpose. The fact is that we operate better when we are connected to something or someone beyond ourselves. Retirees that continue to work after retirement at age 70, whether part-time or full-time, have a life expectancy two and a half times longer than those that don't work. This has much to do with being part of something grander than themselves. The above thought could be said about people who volunteer at different organizations as well.

Studies have shown that when a person retires without significance within a community, it is a predictor of the quality and the quantity of years after retirement. We were created for purpose and after we are done working we can lose it if work was our purpose and our significance. People who can't wait to do nothing in retirement but sit around and do some chores will most likely meet an earlier end than they need to. Whether you are a Christian who believes the Bible or you are completely secular, you need community to stay thriving in life.

In a study about plaque buildup and cholesterol, rabbits were pumped full of cholesterol to study how they were affected. The rabbits were put into cages and stacked on top of one another. The rabbits on the lower tiers fared better than the ones on the higher tiers. Why? The lab person likes rabbits and would pet the ones she could reach, which were the lower tiers. The lower tiered rabbits had 60 percent less plaque. The researchers switch the rabbits from the top to the bottom and from the bottom to the top and again the bottom ones. The ones of the bottom began to improve. There was no doubt about it, touching and patting the rabbits was the difference maker.[4]

There are plenty of studies that seem to declare that community matters to our physical and mental health. People who have had a heart attack were four times more likely to have a second heart attack if they lived an isolated life than their connected brethren. When you are going through a life-threatening disease, you stand to live twice as long if you are a part of a support group. Unmarried men are twice as likely to die of a heart attack. "The angriest men have about four times the mortality rate after heart attacks as the happiest guys. Go home to an empty house after your first heart attack and you double the risk of having a second heart attack within a few months. Having close friends predicts survival, and the more connected, the higher the survival rate."[5]

If our purpose only goes as far as we can reach, in other words if life is all about us, we will never operate maximally as human beings. We will never reach the years that we could have reached. We will never attain our destiny. At the lecture I attended by Dr. Caroline Leaf (the brain scientist), she said that when we think and behave with self-interest as our number one priority, our brains do not operate at their potential. That is crazy, but it doesn't surprise me. We weren't designed to be selfish. That is one of the motives that destroy us and it will destroy cultures and nations. Selfishness is a terrible thing.

I am not saying that we can't do things for ourselves. I work out five days a week for an hour or more. That takes time away from many things and it's spent on just me. Not really just me. If I am healthy and de-stressed, if I have endorphins and happy messengers running through my body, I am a better me for my family, my friends and my job. The benefits of the things you do for yourself should have a ripple effect towards others. We can dishonestly use that as an excuse to be self-centered or we can get real and understand the ripple concept. I go away every year for two nights to plan the next year of life; it is just me, my iPad and God. Well, I bring my surfboard too. It is my time to get God's vision for the year about what things I need to concentrate on, change or continue. It is my God time. The effects of that time are not just ripples; they are waves. Make sure that your "me time" has the ripples that will positively affect those around you.

Community Killers

Let's take a look at some practical things that keep us from getting to our next level in relationships.

Offenses

While in Israel I once heard an Israeli say, "You Americans are so easily offended that you can't even laugh at yourselves." We are so quick to get offended. If someone looks sideways at us we assume that they have ill will towards us when they really were just trying to adjust their contact lens. The other side of this is that we were truly offended. Someone hurt us—bad.

> We construct walls when we are hurt to safeguard our hearts and prevent any future wounds. We become selective, denying entry to all we fear will hurt us. We filter out anyone we think owes us something. We withhold access until these people have paid their debts in full.[6]

The problem with that is that they rarely, if ever, pay their debts to us. We are forever holding a grudge against them, even if they are back in our lives.

Solution: Let it go, real or imagined. If you need to talk to that person, pull them aside and tell them how that made you feel. You will know soon enough if they are friend or foe. Go into that time deciding to forgive and let it go. Make sure your security and worth as a person are not tied to them or anyone else who can crush you. Anchor yourself in God. He never changes His love is for you. It may not be easy, but it must be done or that will have ripple effects on every other relationship.

Unforgiveness and Bitterness

The Bible talks about a "bitter root" that will grow up to defile many (Hebrews 12:15). Unforgiveness properly turns into bitterness and affects all of you and the people around you. You may think that you can contain your bitterness to a person, or two or three, but you can't. It will end up growing to affect every relationship you have including the one with yourself.

Bitterness affects body chemistry, which is dangerous. People that hold onto bitterness have prolonged elevated cortisol levels, which will cause havoc in your systems, including but not limited to your immune system. Simply put, prolonged cortisol elevation mitigates your body's ability to fight off disease. This equates to: bitterness equals physical sickness. But wait, there is more. If your body chemistry is thrown off and your blood pressure is raised as well as your protein levels (such as C-reactive protein), that can take a toll on your heart and other parts of the body. As well, your mood is definitely altered by your own decision to remain bitter and therefore your brain chemistry is thrown off balance. That in turn causes more inability to think correctly and can lead to PTED (post-traumatic embitterment disorder), and also raises the chance for depression. I have heard it said that being bitter toward someone is like drinking poison and expecting someone else to die. It is not worth it.

Solution: Forgive. There is no easy way to forgive when you have been hurt. It is a decision of your will and may need to be rehearsed for quite some time until you can look at that person and not think of hurt or what they did. Forgiveness is not saying, "What you did is okay," it is instead saying, "You are out of my punishment cell." Maybe, if the occurrence is horrendous, they need some reckoning. Let God take care of that.

Resentment

Resentment settles in like a squatter in the forest of bitter roots that have grown up into sprigs. Resentment is poison to us, and like bitterness it cannot be contained. It is a liquid that seeps through the pores of the most closely molecular bonded containers. This will no doubt produce betrayal as a natural consequence. Everyone will become your enemy.

Solution: Forgive. You may also want to begin to bless that person. I'll give you a key to the Kingdom of God. If there is a line that goes from minus 100, to zero, to plus 100 and your resentment is at negative 50, then obtaining a zero isn't enough. It won't even get rid of your resentment or anything else. Besides, who wants to be a zero? You have to go over the line at least to plus 50. To move to the plus side of the scale you can't just release resentment, you have to bless and love, which is where you want to be.

Jealousy

Jealousy is defined as wanting what you don't have. It never enjoys when good things happen to others. Usually, all it wants is what it wants and when others get what jealousy wants, hatred appears. Then the cycle of imbalance to brain, body and relationships spirals downward.

Solution: Decide to accept where you are and set your sites on greater things for yourself. Jealousy, like so many things, means you have your eyes on others. A focus on God and His plan and purpose for your life, with contentment, allows you to be happy for the blessings others receive. Contentment doesn't mean that you stop striving for greatness; it means that you are satisfied and thankful with what God has given you. You may be in a place that is not God ordained and you should never be satisfied or content there. However, to focus on how others are better off than you is a trap that keeps you where you are.

Hatred

Hatred is maybe the strongest word, and a powerful emotion. It is not quite the antithesis to love. There is too much strong emotion involved in it. Hatred, as mentioned before, ruins your very DNA. We cannot contain hatred without experiencing problems at every level and in every area of life. It produces the very effect that if you had an enemy—which you do—he would love to see.

Solution: Surrender. Books are written about this subject and they all come to the same conclusion: you have to surrender your hatred. Finding out where it comes from or why it persists is fine, but the bottom line is: surrender your right to hate. When you hate, you lose.

Isolation

Sometimes we isolate because of hurt. The problem with that is it becomes woven into the fabric of our lives. That is who we become: isolated. Whether we are around people or physically isolate, we are away. We are distant. It is a decision of change that we made in the past that took effort, strength and ability. After a while it became automatic. It has become part of our culture. It is no wonder the divorce rate is where it is today. Our hearts are becoming broken and numb and whatever we are doing isn't fixing the problem.

Solution: Risk. A friend of mine wrote a book about it: *The Risk Factor: Crossing the Chicken Line Into Your Supernatural Destiny.* You have to cross it. You have to step out and allow people the right to hurt you.[7] That isn't easy, but you can't have love without it. There is no easy fix, no baby step to make. There is connecting and there is not connecting.

All the solutions above could be looked at as simplistic. They are. Many of the answers or solutions that we are looking for are simple. However, they can be difficult to embrace. Some people do need some psychological help to get them to the solution or to the point of being able to look at the solution, but most of us will not. Most of us have to learn to deny our feelings and do what we know is best. We know it will work. Somewhere deep inside of us we want to do it, but there is that other part, that brokenness that is trying to take over. We must not be defined by our brokenness, all the while not ignoring that it exists and affects us. What I am saying is, you can do it. You can love again. You can be free from hatred, bitterness and the like. You were designed to love.

Divorce

Divorce doesn't just happen in marriage, it happens everywhere. Whole families are divorced. Family gatherings at Christmas or other times of year are abhorred, or at least not looked forward to. You can divorce in your head and your heart before you do it in reality, which happens most of the time. You can divorce your friends, your kids, your parents and even your church! I once heard a story about a guy who was shipwrecked on a deserted island. One day he was rescued and the captain of the ship came ashore to get the shipwrecked man. The captain noticed three huts and asked the guy why there were three. The guy pointed to one and said, "That one is my house. That is where I stayed. That one there is my church. I go there on Sunday and Wednesday to pray and worship." The captain asked what the last hut could be. The guy calmly answered, that is the church I used to go to—I left.

The culture of divorce is in America. I think it is bred from the time we are adolescents. What do you do with a girlfriend when you don't like her anymore, or you like someone else more than her? You break up. That is divorce. We get mad at childhood friends and that anger lasts long enough to divorce them—forever. We don't know how to fight through rough times in a relationship. We weren't taught to do it. *Get mad. Get even. Get lost. The new American culture.* Marital divorce used to be difficult. You had to prove certain things for it to be granted. Now all it takes is money. The results are the same. Breakage. Tragedy. Fractured lives. A piece of your heart missing.

Various studies on the US rate of divorce show significant differences when a comparison is made in first, second and third marriage breakups in America. The marriage breakup rate in America for first marriages is 41-50%; the rate after second marriage is from 60-67%; and the rate for third marriages is as high as 74%. Reports also say that couples with children have a slightly lower rate of breakup as compared to couples without children. This is due to the fact that being childless is one of the prime causes behind divorce in America. Also, the children of divorced parents are prone to divorcing four times more than the children of couples who are not divorced.[8]

Friendship

> [9]*Two are better than one, because they have a good return for their labor:* [10]*If either of them falls down, one can help the other up. But pity anyone who falls and has no one to help them up!* [11]*Also, if two lie down together, they will keep warm. But how can one keep warm alone?* 12*Though one may be overpowered, two can defend themselves. A cord of three strands is not*

quickly broken. (Ecclesiastes 4:9–12)

Sharing fun is better than having it on your own. Going through hard times with someone is easier than going through it alone. We need to share those moments, whether joy or pain with somebody. It could be a relative, a friend or a spouse, but we operate better when we are connected. There is just something about being able to call a close friend, family member or spouse and tell them some good news.

Remember *Rambo* (the movie)? Johnny Rambo was the consummate warrior and needed nobody. He could take on the entire Russian army and win—with a bow and arrows. Remember him sowing up a big gash on his arm—by himself?[9] Well, I am here to tell you that only Rambo can do it alone. Everything is better with someone by your side.

I think about the few surgeries that I had; how could I have made it alone? I am sure that I could have. I am a strong individual. I can take care of business. But things like putting my shoes on or taking a sponge bath and washing my hair in the sink after ACL reconstruction would have been extremely difficult. Sure, I could have done it, but I am positive that my wife and kids moved my recovery along.

I will never forget Russell Crow in *Gladiator* when he and the others were thrown into the stadium together to reenact the battle of Carthage. They were supposed to die. The chariots came in with the seasoned warriors on them and Russell Crow told all the men to act as one. Nobody was supposed to separate from the group. One guy did—he died. Maximus (Russell Crow) yelled, "As one," and all of them came together in formation. Together they defeated the experienced, better-equipped warriors that were supposed to easily kill them.[10] Their strategy? Connectedness.

Being a part of like-minded people who improve our ability for success is just plain smart. We know this in business. We get around people who will help our success and we can help their success as well. We meet regularly for lunch or breakfast to spur each other on. Ideas are exchanged and there is some kind of camaraderie that keeps us coming back. It isn't for the sales leads, it is for the community.

Whatever you like to do, join a group of hikers, runners, travelers, or whatever! We have this thing at our church that I really hope catches on. It is called "Doing Life." We figure that many people have certain interests, like working out at the gym, in common. So when you are going to work out, you post on the Facebook wall in our "Doing Life Group" that you are going to the gym, what type of workout you're doing, and what time you'll be there. It could be a movie premier, or hiking, or whatever; we decided to do it together. Don't be like the person who invented the back scratcher. You know that guy was lonely!

Children

> [7]*Again I saw something meaningless under the sun:* [8]*There was a man all alone; he had neither son nor brother. There was no end to his toil, yet his eyes were not content with his wealth. "For whom am I toiling," he asked, "and why am I depriving myself of enjoyment?" This too is meaningless—a miserable business!* (Ecclesiastes 4:7–8)

Having eight children has given me a distinct advantage in life. There have been things that I have had to incorporate into the fabric of our family because of its size. For instance, we can't back down from our demands on our children as parents. If we do, and the kids sniff it out, we would have a mutiny and the patients would be running the asylum. Tongue in cheek aside, I really do have an advantage. I have had to think long and hard about why I do what I do. I have had to evaluate my time and energy and where I put my focus. There have been times that sweeping correction has been demanded of me by my family—that's a good thing. These are the most important people in my life and they deserve my best. They haven't always had it. I have failed them at times. Long hours. Distracted presence. Goalless living. That is where course corrections come in. We can't throw in the towel because we have failed here and there or failed miserably. We make the corrections and get to the business of parenting.

My children will be a compilation of Terry (myself) plus Lora (my wife) no matter what I do. They will learn and take on my traits as well as hers. My hope and my goal is for them to add an overwhelming helping of Jesus into that formula. It is my job to teach, instruct and demonstrate healthy relationships in every area. The science of epigenetics even tells us that the change that hatred can make in my DNA can be passed down to my children genetically. They will still have a choice in the matter, but they will have a marker of sorts—a dormant predisposition. Oh, God, help us! How we live matters to our kids all the way down to our DNA.

Our kids need our love. They need our approval. Every young man needs to know that he has what it takes and every young woman needs to know that she is enough. It is their heart's cry and needs to be said—over and over again. If I had a nickel for every time I heard the phrase, "Daddy, watch me," I would be rich. I have heard it at least 100,000 times. I am rich. You, Mr. or Mrs. Parent, have the ability to speak into your child like nobody else can. You can give them the value and security that they so desperately need and point them to God who is our ultimate value. They are waiting for you. Holding their breath. Tell them that they are great. Convince them.

Maybe you are reading this and you don't have children. Well, adopt some. I am not saying that you need to go through a legal adoption. There are plenty of orphaned kids, or children with absent parents, that need a role model. Deadbeat dads are rampant in our culture. If you are a man, you have more opportunities than you know to become a mentor to a young man. When I was growing up, I needed one badly. My youth pastor spent hours and hours with me, but it wasn't until another man, Dave Pocoroba, came into my life that I understood what it was to be a father. Dave was a fun, adventurous tough guy. He taught me how to box, and he taught me how to spear fish. We spent hours studying the Bible, and Charles Spurgeon, and even wrote a play based on C.S. Lewis' *The Screwtape Letters*. Most of all, Dave corrected me. I needed a lot of correction. I was a 19-year-old know-it-all who hadn't been honed much at all. Dave honed me. He loved me so I kept coming back after he would have another thing to say that I needed to correct. I would be first in line at the church potluck and would pile my plate full with three helpings of food so I wouldn't have to go back for more. When Dave got done with me, I ate last. It is a practice that I have kept all these years unless I am being honored with a first place. Three intense years with Dave turned me into a man. I could never repay him.

You can be a Dave Pocoroba in somebody's life. There are young people who need your love, care and the tutelage that you can bring. You were designed to give away what you have toiled for your whole life. Your wisdom and experience needs to be passed down. Find someone. Go.

Marital Love

The silver screen, and now the 55" inch LED screen, has taught us a few things about love. First of all, lovers are rarely married. Think about it. Second of all, it has taught us about happily ever after, which is a myth. In fact, the sunset that people ride off into quickly turns into dark and then into another day. That day brings forth another battle that needs to be won. Thankfully, we are made to battle together, side-by-side, to slay the dragons of this life. But the thought that at the wedding ceremony, the battle is over, is non-sense. The reality is: that was the end of the first round.

Marriage is one of the best inventions of our Creator. It is unbelievably satisfying and will produce many more things than children. Being married brings a completeness to our lives that we were searching for. If you are not married today and have been waiting, don't give up. If you are married today, decide that your marriage is going to be the greatest on the planet. There are so many things that you can do to make it great, but the first is to love. Loving deep and pure will bring such life to a marriage, or to any relationship. Enjoy one another, do the things you did when you first fell in love. Go on dates, get physical, have fun and stop to smell the roses. If there are issues, address them head on. If you need a counselor, go to one and listen to his or her advice. Do what it takes. Your marriage is supposed to be the most satisfying relationship on this earth. God wants it to be that way so He is committed to seeing that through. Join Him.

Not only have we been sold a bill of goods when it comes to marriage and how it doesn't last or doesn't matter, I think the wrong view of love has almost been bred into us. It happens to us like doubt happens in the absence of faith. In the absence of real love, our God-given love has been supplanted by this counterfeit love. It surely includes sex, which may be an expression of erotic love, or a romantic love, but that isn't all there is to love! There is so much more. That is like saying water (H_2O) is one molecule of hydrogen. That is so wrong! It has two molecules of hydrogen and one molecule of oxygen. In fact, isn't it the blending of those base molecules in the periodic table that brings us sustenance, beauty and enjoyment? So let's do a quick check on what real love, God's type of love is:

> [4]*Love is patient, love is kind. It does not envy, it does not boast, it is not proud.* [5]*It does not dishonor others, it is not self-seeking, it is not easily angered, it keeps no record of wrongs.* [6]*Love does not delight in evil but rejoices with the truth.* [7]*It always protects, always trusts, always hopes, always perseveres.* (1 Corinthians 13:4–7)

This beautiful passage has been read many times, especially at weddings. It is poetic. It is wonderful. It is Godly love. So let's see how you do. How does it play out in real life?

I want you to think about a person whom you love. Maybe it is your spouse or your child or just a good friend. Do you have that person's name? Now read these points taken from the above passage and put their name in the blank.

- I love _____ patiently and endure the difficulties of our relationship.
- I display kindness to _____ and provide beneficial things to him/her.
- I do not have strong envy and resentment against _____ or have intense negative feelings over _____'s achievements or success. I am happy when _____ succeeds.
- I don't brag about myself to _____ lifting myself up so they feel small.
- I don't act shamefully around _____ doing things or saying things that are morally indecent.
- I just don't think about my own good around _____ using them for my own benefit or thinking about myself first in the relationship.
- I don't get irritated around _____ and how they act doesn't cause me to become emotionally aroused in a

negative sense.

- I don't keep any records of the wrong things, evil things or the harm that _____ has done to me.
- I don't get happy when _____ has wrong things happen to them or by them.
- I like getting together with _____ and I enjoy telling _____ the truth (with love).
- I always put up with annoyance and difficulty with _____ .
- I always have faith in _____ and trust him/her.
- I always look forward with confidence to that which is good and beneficial in the life of _____ .
- I always continue to bear up with _____ despite difficulty and suffering.

How did you do? Do you have some ground to cover still? Most do. I have a feeling you are probably doing a decent job at loving someone who is close to you and that you really do love them. Hopefully you can see where you need to step it up. I put my wife's name in those blanks and I am looking pretty good. Not perfect, but you would think I honestly love her. Where could you improve? What could be better? Everyone has to start somewhere. Start where you are and decide that you are going to be better at loving others.

Now comes the twist to see if you really understand what love is like and what you are like. Do you require yourself to really love people or just sort of love them? Now think of the person that is a little harder for you to like. Hopefully it isn't the same person as above! Think of a difficult child or a friend or even a parent. Put their name in the blank. Go through the list again.

Love has a lot of components; but we know that. It is good to look into the mirror and make sure that we are not cheating the love we have for one another. Community is built on love. It is the mutual care and love for one another that spurs our hearts onward. We are healthier. We are happier. We enjoy life more, and we are able to aspire to greater things. Studies show all of it. People who are in community are just better off. So love deeply, get in community and enjoy a better life.

10

Financial Part of the Whole

It was years ago, a couple of years into my marriage, that I made a decision. We were not going to buy a home or drive nice cars because my wife was not going to work full time. We were not going to be bringing in enough money to have those things, so I lost the vision for living well, living abundant monetarily. I wanted to live in abundance like most people, but somehow I had figured that we would never attain it. I knew we would be taken care of and have all of our needs met and I was satisfied at that level.

Fast-forward about 20 years. I was camping with my family, I think eight of us were there, and I was watching my kids play and a couple of them were riding the bikes that we brought along. I always loved camping, especially at Twin Lakes near Mammoth in California. I grew up camping here with my parents and they are the fondest memories that I have of our family being together. I don't remember what caught my eye or what I was thinking when I said, "I'll never be able to afford that." It was then that I nearly heard God with my own ears. It was such a loud voice inside of me that it quickened my attention and elicited a response. What God said revolutionized my life in regards to finances.

This wasn't a moment of prayer or internal reflection; I was just hanging out saying what I have said for years. In fact, I regularly said that I would never be able to afford this or that. I often rehearsed the phrase, "We are broke." At Twin Lakes God said, "I can't do anything with that kind of thinking." The world stopped. I was focused on what I just heard loud and clear. "I can't do anything with that kind of thinking." I knew what the "that" was; it was the "I'll never have…" thinking. I was stunned. I felt a little undone; like I got caught with my hand in the cookie jar—by God. How long had He been saying this before I finally heard it? It wasn't like I was doing anything wrong or immoral. So I thought. My thinking, which determined my belief system about money, had led me to my mediocre finances. My thinking about my own potential had left me wanting most of the time. I had settled. Worse than that, I thought my attitude about money was "holy."

Maybe your thinking has gotten you into trouble or it has kept you *under the circumstances*. Our thinking determines how we spend money and what we will make or attain financially. We all have philosophies on how much we can make, how much we give, what kind of stuff we will have, how we will spend and what money is for in the first place.

Some may think that finances aren't really a part of who they are. Your spiritual self, or your physical self, or your emotional self, and other areas are all self-evident, but this one is a bit disconnected from who we are as people, right? Finances are a big stressor for many people and it is in the top three reasons that people divorce. In many parts of the world and particularly in the west, it is of great importance to most and greatly affects the way we live. Whether the economy is good, fair or downright bad, we need to have a handle on our finances, or they will handle every other area of our life. So let's take an honest look at this important area.

First, we have to come to a philosophy about the purpose of finances. What is money for? What is the purpose of making a living? What is the purpose, if any, to prosper or to live in abundance? Is abundance so I can drive $100,000 cars or so I can travel? Is money evil and to be avoided? Finally, is looking at how God views finances the first step of creating our philosophy about money or an afterthought? You might say it is obvious, but I don't think it is. If it is an easy answer, most don't act on their philosophy.

Just like you don't have to wait to get healthy until you get sick, you don't have to wait to focus on your money until it is all gone. You have the power to control your financial future to a large extent. You are the greatest influencer at the very least.

Your Supply

I suppose we could be fed by ravens and live in a vegetable garden that God himself tended to, but that is not the case for us. We are partners in the majority of our supply. There are times that the heavens open up and financial blessings pour out unexpectedly, but for the most part we work, spend, buy, sell, save and give. The finances that we earn or that are at our disposal are for us to live on, and are used to buy food, clothes and shelter. Our finances are used to pay the bills and to buy things that will help better our lives, like a car or an oven. Simply put, money buys things that you need. I must caution here not to think that money supplies what we need, because it doesn't. The Bible says that God gives us the strength and know-how to earn the money that buys things that we need. God is our supplier no matter how you look at it.

Training

Handling money trains us. It is essential that we learn how to say no to ourselves, to live within boundaries, and to work hard and value what we have. Money teaches us dependence on God and a hard work ethic. It is primary to save for the winter. Maybe we don't understand this principle any longer because we not only see very little difference from summer to winter but also because our jobs are not seasonal and we can get nearly every fresh fruit or vegetable any time of year. Still the principle of preparation needs to be honed, and finances do just that. Finances also teach us not to eat our seed for the next crop. Again, this is a value that has passed most of us by, but if you ate all your seed as a farmer, you would have nothing to plant in the next season. You had to save some of your seed in order to keep your farm going. Money is the same way. When we spend it all, we will soon run into trouble, even if it is in your 60s or 70s when you want to retire and can't without living on the street.

We need to train our children how to handle money. Handling money isn't for the mature; it is for the babe. Teaching them the value of giving, saving and working hard will stick with them throughout their lives. Some years ago I was asked to perform a wedding in Hawaii. I thought it would be a great time for Lora and I to have some alone time in paradise. The couple would allow us to stay at their condo that they rented out, so I just had to get there. The kids heard about the trip and wanted to go. I said, of course...not. That would be quite an expensive trip, so I told them they could go if they earned their own plane fare. They did. We did pay for the youngest two (who were four and six at the time), but the rest of them (from nine to twenty) earned $250 for their plane ticket. They vacuumed people's homes, washed cars, walked dogs, denied themselves of the movies, or bowling, or a Slurpee and saved like crazy. You know what happened? They were really proud of themselves. Not in a bad way, but in a good way. They had confidence with finances. They knew if they worked hard and had God's blessing, that they could handle it. It was a priceless lesson.

It is so easy to want that next gadget instead of allowing the Giver of life to determine how we spend His money. Yes I said His money— Him, as in God. All of it is His and just in case you don't think so, just think how fast you could lose it all and you couldn't do a thing about it. The stock market crashes and you not only lose your portfolio, but you lose your job. Your bank is closed because it has gone belly up and you have nothing to pay your house payment with except to sell all your possessions. I'll stop there before fear sets in and I'll encourage you to let trust settle in. If all the money and possessions that are under your management are His, then He has the obligation to take care of them. I know that good, God-fearing people go through financial hardships sometimes, but they always come out of it better. That is because all of what they have is God's. It is quite freeing when you think about it.

> So if you have not been trustworthy in handling worldly wealth,
> who will trust you with true riches? (Luke 16:11)

Talk about training grounds! The most important things in life cannot be bought or sold. True riches are so far beyond anything that you could hold in your hands or see on a balance sheet. The most important training school about money is that if we can tame that dragon, we will inherit true riches. Look at it this way: if you are all about the mighty buck, then you can't possibly be all about loving people. That doesn't mean you can't work hard or even be extremely successful and love people, it means that money and material possession can't have a hold on you without choking the life out of you. If the life is choked out of you, how will you give away the most important things in life? As Bob Dylan said in his song "Gotta Serve Somebody," you can either serve the devil or God. He should have added you can serve yourself, but the fact remains, you serve someone. The love of money (not money itself) is the root of all kinds of evil. If that is your master, then all else in your life will bow to it.

Others

Money isn't just for us. If we acquire things solely for ourselves, we have missed the point of this life. Just like our life and our love, finances are to be shared. They are to be given away. Why do you think that God would want us to be in abundance if it is not to be His supply arm to others? Financial abundance is supposed to overflow towards others. Sure, you save an inheritance for your children (they qualify as others), and you can also give them the lesson of a lifetime about money by giving. It is better to give than to receive. Actually, it is immensely more satisfying to give. To know that you are a part of something more than yourself is gratifying. It is in our human code. When we are only about ourselves, well... you know people like that. Don't you love to hang around them? Giving inspires us and it must be our philosophy to give regularly.

Enjoyment

Some have such a struggle with enjoying money. Does God really give us finances for our enjoyment? Yes!

Command those who are rich in this present world not to be arrogant nor to put their hope in wealth, which is so uncertain, but to put their hope in God, who richly provides us with everything for our enjoyment. (1 Timothy 6:17)

Of course we are supposed to enjoy ourselves. When you bought your child their first bike (or when you will in the future), did you get it for them so they could have transportation or that they would enjoy it? Of course they would use it at some point to get to their friends house, or to church, or the ball field, but you got it for them so they could enjoy riding it. It was a gift of love that would be used for enjoyment and for purpose. God is the same way. He wants us to enjoy what we have—why wouldn't He?

Mindsets

Some are content to have very little possessions, which can be good. Some think they only deserve or will only ever *just make it*, while others strive their skin off to get ahead and have the *good life*— whatever that is. Based on our adjusted view of the purpose of money none of the above mindsets are right. In fact, these mindsets give birth to bondage. Before we get into that, we must answer the question that Time Magazine posed on September 18, 2006: "Does God Want You To Be Rich?"

Let's let God answer this question:

The blessing of the Lord makes one rich, and he adds no sorrow with it. (Proverbs 10:22 NKJV)

The Hebrew for blessing in this verse is *berakah*, which means abundance. The Hebrew for the word rich is *ashar*, which means accumulation or to cause to grow rich. Thus, the transliteration (literal translation) of the first half of Proverbs 10:22 is this: "Abundance from God is to give you accumulation to cause you to grow rich. Does that leave any room for doubt about God's intentions toward us with regard to the topic?"[1]

It is hard to believe with over 2000 verses in the Bible about money, with all the instruction about money, with all the promises of abundance and with everything that Jesus spoke in regards to provision, that anyone could come up with another answer. God has abundance and loves to give it away.

And my God will meet all your needs according to the riches of his glory in Christ Jesus. (Philippians 4:19)

The question is, what is rich? How much do you need before you are considered rich? The middle class in the west is rich. There, I said it. We may not have a Cigarette boat or a Maserati, but compared to most of the world we are rich. In fact, if we didn't spend so much, we would be rich enough to do the things that we consider only rich people can do. We have so much at our fingertips. We are incredibly blessed. I know there are people that are hurting financially, but the vast majority of us are very well off. It has been a fantastic blessing, and it has proven to be a large stumbling block. Are some then not supposed to be rich? Good question.

When you begin to trust in riches or when you begin to be an insatiable acquirer of goods, riches have become your undoing. A question was asked of the top CEO's in the country, "What is your biggest regret?" The number one reply was that they regret not spending enough time with their families. When we chase riches, we lose perspective of everything else. I am not saying don't work hard, but there must be a limit to our working. We are not purposed to be ladder climbing, money-making machines. We have a divine purpose so much deeper than that. If you are in that trap, get out. Do whatever you need to do, including selling things and downsizing to get out of the trap of making life about earnings.

Yet after saying this, the answer to the question does God want us to live in abundance is a resounding yes. Some of us are just not ready for that blessing and I pray it doesn't come until you are ready to handle it. Our life is so much more than worldly riches, I get that, but that doesn't mean we shouldn't have them or believe for them. We need to get to our own personal next level in finances. Don't settle for mediocre.

Mediocre Mindset

Mediocre is like treading water and just keeping your head above water. Most of us have used that phrase to describe how we are doing.

The problem with treading water is that you are going nowhere, except towards exhaustion. This mindset kills us. We work, and work, and work and get nowhere because we figure that we aren't supposed to go anywhere except retire and live on social security. Good luck with that. Mediocre is sin. I don't think that is in the Bible, but you could write it in your margin. Mediocre brings death to our dreams from childhood, or even the dreams of our teens and early twenties. Something happened along the way. We got discouraged, we chose the wrong career path, we made big spending mistakes, or we just lost hope and now we figure that this is our lot in life—so-so-ness.

Poverty Mindset

> *The enemy of "the best" is not "the worst." The enemy of the "the best" is "just fine."*[2]

Then there's the poverty mindset, which has two sides to it. The first side says that it is "all okay." "Everything is just fine." "I don't need to have more than I have, which isn't much." This mindset believes that mediocre is good enough and anything else would be more than what is deserved. There is this awkward comfort with having less than. The second side is the poor me, give me what you have mentality. It wants things from others that haven't been earned. It says that I have been handed a rotten hand and you have a good one, so give me some cards. Both of these mentalities are success killers. You will never experience abundance if you don't break out of these mentalities. It is time to have a heart-to-heart talk with yourself and answer the begging question: Do I have or even come close to having the poverty mindset?

So how do you break out of the poverty or mediocre mindset? Change your mind and change your heart. First you have to believe that you are not a victim to any circumstances. Whatever hurdles and challenges that life has dealt you, you will overcome them and be stronger for it. You can be more than you are now. You have what it takes. You have to be happy for and inspired by other people's success instead of being jealous of it. You want to get close to them not for any kind of handout, but for a transfer of their healthy mentally. Whenever you get rid of a mindset or a way of thinking, you have to replace it.

You have to fill the void so to speak. Just like in the other chapters, you have to start declaring the corrected mindset. Your mind has to be renewed and your ears have to hear your mouth saying it. You have to pull out the engine that was in your car and put a completely new one under the hood.

The second thing is your heart has to change. Your heart has a brain and it is programmed to judge truth and make decisions. Your heart needs a change. Your core beliefs have to come into agreement with what God says about you.

> For God is the one who provides seed for the farmer and then bread to eat. In the same way, he will provide and increase your resources and then produce a great harvest of generosity in you. (2 Corinthians 9:10 NLT)

> [1]Blessed is the one who does not walk in step with the wicked or stand in the way that sinners take or sit in the company of mockers. 2But whose delight is in the law of the Lord, and who meditates on his law day and night. 3That person is like a tree planted by streams of water, which yields its fruit in season and whose leaf does not wither—whatever they do prospers. (Psalm 1:1–3)

> [1]Praise the Lord. Blessed are those who fear the Lord, who find great delight in his commands. [2]Their children will be mighty in the land; the generation of the upright will be blessed. [3]Wealth and riches are in their houses, and their righteousness endures forever. (Psalm 112:1–3)

That should give you a good start. God wants to prosper you. How much is up to Him and how much is up to you? Believing is the first step. Will you believe God? Will you believe that what He says applies to you? Jeremiah says that God has a plan to prosper you. His *plan* is to prosper you and He has a plan for you to implement to get there.

There is one more thing about this poverty mindset. It wants to get rich quick. "If I could just win the lotto…" If you did, chances are you would wind up like those who have gone before. They don't end up well.

A faithful person will be richly blessed, but one eager to get rich will not go unpunished. (Proverbs 28:20)

Get Rich Mindset

The get rich mentality will keep us concentrating on the wrong thing. Whatever we concentrate on most will become our God. Remember, working is a way to generate income for ourselves and for others. The money that comes from that income serves God, ourselves, our family and others.

One more thing needs to be said plainly here. Money is for God's purposes. If we don't give our money to God our money may become our god. We will tend to trust riches instead of God and work for riches instead of serving God. We won't rely on God and we will become our own god, trusting in ourselves to supply our every need and desire, and we have a lot of desires. That is a hair-raising place to be. Let God be God.

All or Nothing Mindset

We see that many in the churches have a hard time believing for anything beyond getting by and they don't think they deserve anything more than necessity. This keeps them from having the blessing of giving to others, partnering with God Himself to bring provision and love to others. Some in the church put a large emphasis on money and God wanting to bless you. It is taught on a monthly or weekly basis and the idea you get from some is that if we don't drive a sweet ride, live in a huge home, and wear bling that we are missing God's will. Both of these mindsets are wrong.

We have to call in the promises and believe them whole-heartedly. You may be in the middle of a very difficult time right now. God is going to see you through. You may have lived in so-so land for so long you forgot how to dream let alone remember what you used to dream. Dream again. Believe for big things. If you don't believe for anything bigger than you can supply, then your dream isn't a God-sized dream. When you have to endure difficult times, hold on to your dream from God. Things don't always go smoothly, but whether you have some rough times or smooth sailing, God will bring you through. Don't faint and don't give up.

Creating Wealth

Believe for It

The first thing you have to do is believe for it. Begin to speak those verses above and your core beliefs out. Hold on to them like the bracing handle on a rollercoaster after the safety belt came undone. Don't let anyone steal your heart's belief.

Work Hard

Another thing we can do is work hard. Just talking about it, sleeping in, zero planning and no discipline leads to poverty. Get out there and take care of business.

> *All hard work brings a profit, but mere talk leads only to poverty.* (Proverbs 14:23)

I just love the fact that many of my kids worked for me. To be honest, I kicked their little fannies on the job site. I expected hard work and I rewarded them handsomely. Many times I would give them incentive bonuses. They learned how to work hard and to hold their work up to a high level of proficiency. There are things that we must do to give God a chance to bless us. Working hard and doing it well is one of them.

Think High and Outside

Think outside the box. If you grew up and everyone around you went to work for the factory (there is nothing wrong with that) but your dream is bigger than that yet you don't know how to accomplish it, you have got to think differently than those around you. If you are at the factory or a corporation, ask God to promote you and work like you want it. Position yourself for increase. Invent something. The Creator of the universe lives in you so you are by nature creative. So create something. Follow through on all ideas. You just never know when the next thing you think of will be a gadget or software that will sell.

I had a friend that started a record label. He was a painter (house painter) and they were not rich at all. He was just following his dream. It turns out that after he copyrighted his record label that another recording company with the same name wrote him and told him to stop using their name. They had been in business for years. The problem for them was Mike (my friend) had copyrighted the name. He owned it. They had to buy it. They did, with a lot of zeros! You just never know when your dream will explode.

Be a Giver

Giving cannot be overstated. There is a universal law of God that says when you give you gain more. This goes way beyond giving at your local church (if you go to one). We are talking about a lifestyle of giving.

> [24]*One person gives freely, yet gains even more; another withholds unduly, but comes to poverty.* [25]*A generous person will prosper; whoever refreshes others will be refreshed.* (Proverbs 11:24–25)

We don't give to get. That would be self-centered. How, though, can I not consider this principle that is spelled out over and over again in God's Word? I can't. Giving is fun and God does have a prescription on how to give.

1. Don't tell people—in fact it would be good for you to forget it too.
2. Decide what you are going to give and set it aside regularly.
3. Give it with hilarity.

There are more than those, but those are a good start. Develop a giving lifestyle and watch your entire life improve including the fun quotient of giving, even when it is a sacrifice.

Know Where You Are

Know the status of your finances. You have to understand where the money is going. Everyone knows generally where it is going, but only after accounting for it do we understand enough to make changes. After we have an accurate picture, we will know what to work on, where we can cut and how much to increase to position ourselves for success.

Get Specific Vision

After you have figured out why you have money and what it is for, and after you have thought about your future success and understand where you are right now, you are almost ready to embark on a plan. However, there is one thing left before you start crunching numbers: a specific vision.

Proverbs tells us that people without a vision for the future have no restraint. Applying that life principle to money they just spend when they feel like it. When the new gadget comes on the market or that new restaurant opens up or whatever, they spend if they have the money. As I write, I have two things I want to do. The first is to paint my house. My house has needed paint for a while, but the outdoor kitchen took priority. My money and effort went into building that. While it is not totally done, it is done enough to be happy. There are a few more things that need to be finished, but those will take a lot of money and time. Painting the house is next on the agenda, except for this trip to Florida. We have a convention in Orlando that we decided would take priority. So every extra dollar is going to that vacation. It's on purpose. We sat down and decided that convention, and of course Disney World, would be a priority and so would taking the youngest four children on the adventure. That is short-term vision.

You have to get a vision for the short-term and for the long-term. Yes, that includes retirement. There is no way around the fact that you will need money to do things and your options are: 1) you have it to spend, 2) you charge it and likely pay more for it later, or 3) you don't do it. I would suggest the first and third option only. When you have a vision, you can plan for it. When you have no vision, you will either spend wildly or you will plan to spend with no future. You could set up a plan to give, save, invest, and spend with some good percentages like 15%, 10%, 15% and 60% respectively, but that would take incredible discipline that most people don't have without a goal they can see.

My wife and I used to talk about our 5-year and 1-year goals whenever we took a long car trip, like to Grama's house 280 miles away. Where do you want to be in five years? In fact, where do you want to be in 10 years? Where do you want to be next year? What financial goals do you have in the next year? What vacations would you like to take? What major purchases will you need to make? What things in the house need replacing? (In the *TLP: Pursuing Life Workbook,* there are worksheets for you to fill out answering many of these questions.) There are things that need to be thought through before you start your financial trip, like where are you going?

Included in the Vision

Emergency Fund

Save a $1000 emergency fund—I agree with Dave Ramsey.[3] This is an important first step for a number of reasons, not the least of which is you may need it for an emergency. You have to put this money somewhere you will not spend it. Don't have it in a savings fund attached to your checking account that you now know you can overdraw because you have that cushion. Do this first and build momentum and confidence.

Release from Debt

Debt is killing us, both as a nation and as individuals. It weighs on us and strangles us from the inside out. It is a difficult burden to bear and it is to be avoided at all costs. The rippling effect it has on other areas of life cannot be understated. We get physically exhausted trying to keep up with the payments. We are stressed out every time we see the bill and our relationships can easily suffer from any of the above realities.

It is David and Goliath for many people when it comes to debt relief. I have searched for some kind of magic program that eradicates your debt with no pain. I couldn't find one. The good news is that God is for you and His plan for you doesn't include debt. That means He is invested in you paying off your debt.

There are a lot of definitions of debt and many opinions on

whether to have it or not. Let me give you my basic definition. To be in debt means you owe somebody something. Bad debt is debt that cannot be paid off with the sale of the item that you went into debt to buy. In other words, if you car loan is $10,000 and you car is worth $8,000 then that is bad debt. Anything owed on credit cards is bad debt. The reason it is bad is because it has you. It exerts a control on you that you cannot avoid. If your car loan was for $10,000, but your car was worth $15,000, then you could sell your car and get out of debt. I am not suggesting that you go into debt for anything, but the worst possible debt is the kind that you can't get out of by selling that item. Opinions vary on housing debt and auto debt, but the fact is, that is usually not what is weighing down our lives (unless you bought way over your head). It is the bad debt. So let's go after that.

Pay off your debts as fast as possible. Start with your unsecured debt and pay it down by taking your smallest balance first and working hard to pay it off with every extra bit of cash you can use. After you have done that, apply that monthly payment to the next debt and start paying that off with what will be a double payment. You can see the next step with the third debt and so on. This will build momentum and you will start seeing some light. Whatever you do, don't take the payment of the now paid off card and start spending it. Use it to pay off more debt until you are done and then start saving for the things that you used to buy with credit cards or loans.

The same principle should be applied with haste to anything you are upside down on; upside down means that you cannot sell the item to pay the debt. You have got to get yourself out from under these debts first before you attack any others.

Many people just don't have the extra to pay on the debts they have. Here is a list of things that you can consider to help pay off your debts.

- Use unexpected gifts. When the money comes in for your birthday, or anniversary, or you get a bonus from work use it to pay down your debt.
- Tap your savings account—leaving your $1,000 emergency fund intact. You are paying much higher interest than you are gaining in a savings account, so it makes sense to use some savings to pay off your debt.

- Save money by cutting down on expenses. Look at your low priorities (explained in the section below, Make a Plan and Stick To It) and cut them down or get rid of them all together. It may just be for a time, but it will be worth it.
- Work more. Again, this is just for a time. It won't be forever. Find a way to use your talents or even what you like to do to make some extra money. Who knows, you might end up making a career change.
- Shop smart. That doesn't mean that you should wait for the pair of shoes you don't need to go on sale before you buy them. Smart shopping is buying your essentials on sale. It is getting over the need to have name brand stuff and go generic. Smart shopping is buying in bulk and storing. Get creative. Coupon and sale shop but don't buy it if you don't already use it or don't need it. The trap of coupons is you buy things that you never use to get a deal on them.
- Eat at home. Eating out is so much more expensive. Make your lunch and take it with you. Eat a few eggs or some steel cut oatmeal with cinnamon for breakfast. Make three casseroles for the week and freeze them so you don't have to prepare dinner every night. Stop spending your money on convenience eating. Plan ahead and eat at home.
- Hold a garage sale. It is time to get rid of your junk and the stuff you haven't worn or used in years. Not only will you make an extra few bucks, but you will clear out some clutter too!

One last question about debt: why did you go into it in the first place? I know you may say that you bought this or that, but why did you buy it? Most of the time there is a core belief that is propelling us or at least giving us permission to go into debt. You have to find what fuels your debt decisions. I remember early in our marriage that I was the family Santa Clause. I bought the most gifts and the best gifts. If you had me in the gift exchange, you were the luckiest of all the family. The only problem was that I went into debt every Christmas. Why? Because I liked being the big spender and the most extravagant giver. There was something deep in my core about wanting to be accepted and liked by my new family that was off and needed to be corrected. Needless to say,

I don't go into debt during Christmas anymore. So answer the why question and not just the how. It is core and it will help you immensely to stay out of debt once you get out. You will get out.

Retirement

Start early and watch it grow. Have you ever seen a compound interest chart? Oh, the law of sevens at work. It grows like hotcakes at the end of things. The longer you can be at the end the more it will exponentially grow. In other words, start planning and saving for retirement early and you will have more cash when you get there. It is never too late, but if you are over 40 you will have to be more aggressive or retire later. There are plenty of books about this and about investing that you can read. My point here is that you need to include this in your vision.

I need to say something here that is in my own personal framework. I don't believe in retirement. It is not a Biblical concept and it doesn't bode well for most people. When we get to retirement age (which keeps getting higher), we should be thinking about what we want to do with our time without a concern for how much, if any, we will be paid for doing it. I'm thinking surf instructor and I don't care how much I get paid for doing it. I believe that we need a passion to pursue. We were never meant to watch TV all day and do nothing. That is fake enjoyment. We were made to be connected with each other and significantly contribute to our community in one way or another. Helping people ride waves and have fun sounds good to me. Whatever it is, find a passion, connect with others and enjoy the work you do.

Make a Plan and Stick to It

> *Most of the people I know aren't in trouble because they have no money; they're in trouble because they've mishandled the money they have.*[4]

Most of us mean well. We don't buy expensive watches if we can't afford them. In fact, if we are in financial trouble, most of us can't think of much, if anything, that we could sell that we shouldn't have bought. It is the day-to-day stuff, the decision to eat out instead of at home, that gets us into trouble. Although some people do buy the BMW instead of the Honda, most of us make many small decisions that end up putting us at a major disadvantage financially. It is time to make a plan and stick to it. It is time to own up to our mistakes, get some backbone and constrain ourselves. We will reap such a wonderful reward if we do.

> *A budget is people telling their money where to go instead of wondering where it went.* – John Maxwell

When you sit down to write a budget, have your goals before you (if you are married, it is completely necessary for you and your spouse to be unified). If your goals are not written out, write them out and put them where you can see them as you create your spending plan. Your number one goal is to spend according to your mission. That cannot be overstated. Don't spend for your wants; spend with your end game in clear view.

You will find a basic budget sheet and a budget builder in the *TLP: Pursuing Life Workbook*. Work with your actual income (your take home pay). Here are your steps:

1. Start with the essentials (rent/mortgage, utilities, food).
2. Prioritize your non-essentials with a number value of 1–10. (Cable TV and eating out are non-essentials).
3. Add these non-essential items to your budget in order from 1–10.
4. Debt has to be put into the essential category. Don't calculate paying the minimum payment. Set a goal to pay off each debt and calculate how long that will take. It is my strong suggestion that you get out of debt as fast as possible. So aim high.
5. Make sure you calculate those every six-month or irregular expenses in your monthly budget. (This includes: house taxes, car insurance, etc.)
6. Make it doable. If this is a pie-in-the-sky plan, then start over and make it doable. If you have a family of four and your food budget is $50.00 per week, I hope you know how

to make a good casserole with dog food. Be realistic.

7. Go back and make necessary adjustments to bring things into balance. If you have more days in the month left at the end of the money, then you are going to have to reduce your spending or increase your income.

This is not rocket science and you don't have to be superman (or superwoman) to do it. You can do this. God is on your side. Go back and make adjustments starting with the lowest number on your prioritized spending list and move up until it comes into balance. If you have cut all you can cut and you still can't make it, then get to praying and dreaming. There is a way for you to make it.

Jesus hasn't returned yet. Pay your bills, take care of business. Get back in the game.[5]

Ask God what to do and do it. If He says move jobs, then move. If He says get a second job for a while, get one. If He says to ask for a promotion, ask for one. If He says sell your car and get a cheaper one, do it. If He says find a place to rent that is less money, move. Finally, if you are still stuck, ask for help—from someone with wisdom and that won't condemn you. You need some inspiration and sometimes you need someone else to give it to you. They will have another perspective because of where they sit. Try it. This is doable!

If you created your spending plan and you have plenty left over even after you have saved, invested, and thought through retirement, there are two things that I would suggest for you to do. First, start dancing! You are blessed and you should be expressing some joyful thanksgiving right now. Second, consider giving more. I have these friends (Dr. John and Barb) that have a Jesus Fund. The Jesus Fund is for people who are in need. They put money in this fund and then when they hear of a need, they often help or satisfy the need. (Especially if Grama Barb gets to shop at Wal-Mart and buy stuff.) They are some of the most giving people I know. I love their Jesus Fund! Consider setting up something like that or drill a water well in Africa, or whatever. Have fun giving. Be a conduit of resource from Heaven to earth, from God to people. Consider the fact that it is why you are blessed, to be God's hand of giving.

11

Making the Change

You have what it takes. You are able to make the choices necessary to change. You have the will to put forth effort and you have the strength within you to summon. I trust after you have read the preceding chapters, you have begun to develop a next-level mentality. Where you are in life may be a good place, but you have come to realize that there is more. You know you have more potential and you can attain a greater destiny. You get there step by step.

In the movie *What About Bob?* (nearly a cult classic in my wife's family), Bob had some serious problems. His psychologist (played by Richard Dreyfuss) had written a book, *Baby Steps*. Bob, (Bill Murray) followed his therapist on vacation and ruined it. However, in the process, he experienced some great breakthrough by taking baby steps. He would say it all the time, "baby steps, baby steps, baby steps."[1] It's a pretty funny movie, and it makes my point here. Take baby steps. You don't have to have it all next week. Things will take time. Implement one thing at a time and concentrate on that until you are ready to move on. When you try to master everything at once you end up becoming mastered.

Let me give you an example of how you can evolve into a different person by taking baby steps. Let's say you have trouble with boundaries. You basically let people walk all over you. Some people would tell you to stop it and take charge. That's easy for them to say. They are able to set clear boundaries. Here are some baby steps to complete freedom. Look at the list below and determine where you are on it. Then look at your next level (the next step on the list). That is your short-term goal. It's your finish line. Until you reach it, then you look at the next one. Baby steps: one level at a time.

- You invite abuse because your boundaries are totally nonexistent.
- Your boundaries exist but are easily violated by anyone.
- You defend a small number of boundaries.
- You establish moderate boundaries and defend them against most incursions, but an experienced predator can still violate your boundaries with impunity.
- You defend your boundaries against all intruders.
- You enlarge your boundaries to reflect a higher level of personal dignity.
- You walk with such authority and dignity that people instinctively respect your boundaries without your actively defending them. There are no more incursions.
- When you are around, predators pull back from everyone without your having to do anything. People are safer and have larger boundaries when they are around you because dominion is so deeply engrained in your spirit.

Celebrate Successes

Look back at your starting point from time to time. If you are using the *TLP: Pursuing Life Workbook* look at the first time you filled out the initial assessment after three months. You will be encouraged as you see that progress is being made. Momentum and successes cannot be forgotten as if they didn't happen. You have to look back every once in a while and say, God has brought me this far, He will take me the rest of the way! Remember that surfboard I was given? Sometimes when finances are tough, when unexpected expenses have come or unexpected drops of income have happened, I think about that surfboard. God blessed me with a surfboard that didn't matter much in the grand scheme of things. If He provided that, He will provide the mortgage payment, house taxes, grocery bill or whatever. The Bible is constantly admonishing us to recount the works of God. When we do, we actually begin to trust because we see that God already came through. We see that God is faithful and that produces faith. So keep talking about those successes. Not like some overweight and out of shape group of guys remembering the glory days of high school football, but recounting how far God has taken you as a propellant to encourage you to keep going.

Change is Inevitable

Change is inevitable, however now you understand that you can control the changes for the better. You get it! Life isn't a river that takes you where it wants to. If you don't like the boat you're in or the river that you are on, get out.

We change when we deem it worthy. Most of us don't like to change. In fact, Robert K. Cooper uncovers in his book, *The Other 90%*, some brain scientists say that the amygdala (located in your brain—it deals with the way you perceive and respond to the world) wants to run our world without change. It craves control and safety and wants you to stay the way you are. We take the same route home every day, we watch the same TV shows, we wash the car in the same fashion...let's face it: we are creatures of habit. When the pain of keeping things the way they are presently is more than the pain of changing, then we change.[2]

When you are diagnosed with something terrible like diabetes, vascular disease or cancer; or when you go through a bankruptcy or lose your job; or when you are threatened with divorce; or you are diagnosed with depression or an anxiety disorder, all of a sudden change is looking pretty good. Why wait until you get sick to become healthy? Why wait for your spouse to threaten divorce to get some help? Why wait until your job is obsolete before getting yourself positioned for a career change? Let's "get 'er done" ahead of time. Why not live in a healthy way and continually reap the benefits of health and wholeness? If you are married, why not enjoy a great marriage? Why not have great friendships? Why not enjoy being joyful?

There is no doubt that you have begun connecting the dots in your own life. Take a few moments to write down what you have observed about your life if you haven't done so already. Assess your life with these questions:

- How has mediocrity, or living below mediocre, hurt you in other areas of life?
- What seems to be the most far reaching problem or issue?
- What problem or issue touches the other areas of your life the most?

Maybe you are completely out of shape or maybe you are living on borrowed money, whatever the issue is, begin to connect the dots to the other areas. How are they affecting each other?

If one is improved will it improve or reflect on another?

First things first, right? Maximize your effort by picking what you need to concentrate on first. Besides closeness with God (I don't know of anything more important than that), I would probably lean toward your thinking, the mental part of you. Of course exercising will improve your thinking, but you knew that already. How you think is so important. It must not be overlooked when you are trying to find where to start or where to focus first.

So...why wait? You know you want the improvement! Thank God if you aren't at some critical point yet. You want to live well, know your purpose in order to live significantly, and not have physical limitation; not now, not ever. You want to stay mentally acute, enjoy life, enjoy others and finish well. Start now and live it.

Making a Plan for Change

Twenty-one days—you can do anything for three weeks! Twenty-one days is your first step. When you repeat the 21-day cycle 3 times, you will have built it into your personhood. It will be a part of you.

Step 1: Decide and Choose to Go for It!

Fill out the "Initial Assessment" in the *TLP: Pursuing Life*

Workbook and when you have completed it, go back and assess it. If you are really serious, have your spouse assess it with you. If your marriage is a bit rocky, that may open up some wonderful communication and insight or it may open up a can of worms. (I advise against it if your spouse is in the anger stage of marital trouble). Get your starting place, first things first. Don't go grandiose or reach for unattainable goals. Keep them doable. If you are 65, don't set your goal to look 25 by working out 3 hours a day. Although if it works, call me and we will write a book together and be kajillionairs. Keep it real.

Step 2: Envision the Next Level

You not only have to envision your end goal, but you have to envision the next level. What does it look like? What does it act like? Not your end game, just the next step. If you are struggling with that, with knowing what your next level is, I encourage you to see yourself down the road in 1-5 years. What do you want to be like? Write it down. Look at it regularly. To determine your next level, work backwards.

I read about a guy who wrote down his five core values. He kept them with him all the time and from time to time would pull out the 3x5 cards they were written on and look at them. That is a person who is serious and focused. You have to see it. Write it down.

Step 3: Plan It – Schedule It – Purpose It – Count the Cost – See the Benefit

You have to put whatever you are going to do into your schedule. To hope it gets done (like wishing) is a trap. Be purposeful and write it down on your calendar—every day. You also have to count the cost ahead of time or you will be in process and may want to stop because it is hard. If you don't count the time and effort it is going to take, it is easy to get discouraged when it takes a little longer than some other things that seemed easy. This takes effort, right? So count the cost and weigh it against the benefit before you start. Be convinced that it is worthwhile.

Step 4: Get a Tool to Track Your Successes

The tool may be a budget sheet or a tape measure (I advise against scales as your physical evaluation tool—weight is deceiving when you are building muscle). Or it may be asking difficult questions to your spouse about how you are doing in certain areas. It may be looking back at your assessment or some other tool. The point here is to have something so you can quantify what is going on. Your goal has to be able to be measured. "Be a better person" is not measurable, but "controlling anger" is if you honestly evaluate how many times you acted in anger in a day. Even if you have to create something yourself, have it on the ready before you begin. Don't be afraid to look at it or be reluctant to track your progress for fear of failure.

Step 5: Be in Community

If applicable, find a group or a couple of friends that are like-minded and have similar types of goals. Obviously you can't have a group for everything, but to hang around some like-minded people would be a fantastic idea. Some of you are going to have to let go of some friendships because they keep you down. Invite them to grow and change with you and if they refuse, then you may have to stop being around them so much for a while. You will be like those you associate with most. So choose well. You could always start a group yourself.

Step 6: Do it! Get in Motion!

Why isn't this number one? You need a field before you play baseball. Otherwise you are just playing catch. However, if you just keep on planning and never do anything you will be like a person who cooks but never eats. Eventually they will stop cooking because they will not have the energy to do so. Plus, the food has already burned, is overcooked or is cold. There is a time to take the turkey off of the BBQ. (We BBQ ours.) There is a time to cook and a time to eat. Get your foot on the gas, put it in first gear and get going.

Step 7: Evaluate Your Progress Every 21 Days

Remember that tool in Step 4? It is time to use it. Have you attained your next level? It is time for an honest evaluation so you know what to do next. Don't rate yourself against anybody else but you. There is no competition here. Where could you have done better? What would have improved your result? If you haven't done very well or haven't stuck to your plan, start again. Don't let setbacks define you. In fact, use setbacks as a springboard to your next success.

Step 8: What's Next?

After you have attained a certain level, decide what is next. Take some time to decide what to focus on next. Don't let a "take a break" syndrome set it. This is life. You are climbing forward. Don't stop the mighty momentum. Take an honest look at your life and make a plan for the next 21 days. Go for it. You have what it takes. Don't let anyone tell you that you don't.

Emmitt Smith was a star athlete in high school but the college and pro scouts said that he was too small and he was too slow to play at the collegiate and pro level. He was reluctantly drafted during his junior year by the Dallas Cowboy's coach Jimmy Johnson who also thought he was too small and too slow and always carried the ball in his left hand. It turned out to be a good pick. The kid who they said wouldn't make it broke the NFL all time rushing yards record, won three Super Bowls and was named MVP of one of them. There is plenty more, but you get the point. They said he couldn't do it, but he did. You can do it. You have what it takes. God is for you and will empower you if you ask Him to. It is time to pursue life totally.

> *For me, winning isn't something that happens suddenly on the field when the whistle blows and the crowds roar. Winning is something that builds physically and mentally every day that you train and every night that you dream.* – Emmitt Smith

12

Planning Your Life

The average workweek hours have increased in the last 20 years.[1,2] However, productivity has risen over 60% according to some,[3,4] yet people are working even more. Still, outside of work there are more activities than ever now. Kids have sports year round, even if it is the same sport. It never stops. Pharmacies are 24-hours now because people can't get there by 5:00 p.m. anymore, or even 10:00 p.m. The growth in the tentacles that are drawing us to spend more time in more places is similar to the growth of the channels available on television. When I was a kid, there were four UHF channels and seven local channels. That was it. Now the small cable or satellite packages are 250 channels. That is what I think has happened to our lives and our expected time expense, it has climbed steadily, nipping at our heals and devouring our best years.

Time wasters have exponentially increased and the ease of those at our fingertips has affected us all.

A recent survey by America Online and Salary.com revealed that the average employee admits to wasting more than two hours every work day. Which activities are eating away at American workers' precious productivity? According to the survey, the top time-wasters include:

Surfing the Web: 44.7 percent
Chatting with co-workers: 23.4 percent
Doing personal business: 6.8 percent
Spacing out: 3.9 percent
Running errands: 3.1 percent
Personal phone calls: 2.3 percent
Applying for other jobs: 1.3 percent
Planning personal events: 1.0 percent

"But I hardly do any of the above," you loudly protest. "I never waste time at work!" The truth is that most people (even you overachieving overachievers) have some bad time habits that eat into your efficiency and effectiveness.[5]

It was years ago that I sat in with a group of people and the subject of our teaching and discussion was time management, planning and scheduling. My eyes rolled not because I had it all sewed up, but because they made it sound so easy. Admittedly it was a difficult area of my life. I could plan my work schedule pretty well, but all of life? Who needed a plan? I had been a successful business owner and father of five before I started pastoring a church and had done just fine. Even while the church was small I did well. However, when the church started to grow and I started to get older it meant statistically (as I have read before and the statistic bears out in my life) I was taking on 5% more responsibility per year after 30. I knew I needed to schedule my life and plan better, but how?

There are the ABC's and the 1-2-3's, the Pareto 80-20 principle, the POSEC Method inspired by Maslow, the A, B, C, D, E from Brian Tracy[6], the four quadrants... and the list goes on. There are charts, graphs, books, apps, software and soon you will be able to put your schedule on the inside of your eye glasses for easy viewing with a shock system to keep you on track. I'd heard about a lot of different methods but I still needed help and something finally clicked when I watched this old video from Steven Covey.[7] The "Ah-ha" moment had arrived.

The video was old, the fashions made me laugh, but the principle I learned is timeless. There were these buckets. One held big rocks and the other held small rocks. The big rocks represented the big things in your life. For me it would be pastor, father, husband, author and so on. The small rocks represented all those things that fill your time during the day. They could be emails, television, Facebook posting and so on. The lady awkwardly dumped all the small rocks into a bucket and then tried to fit in the big rocks. The long and short of the awkwardly long attempt was that she couldn't do it. So she put the big rocks in another bucket and dumped in the small rocks and they all fit. Lesson: first things first—big things first.

Brian Tracy says this with a humorous illustration of eating frogs. In his book *Eat That Frog!*, he talks about eating the biggest frog in the pond first instead of the small ones or the tadpoles. Find the biggest one and eat it one bite at a time.[8] Kinda' gross, but it resonated with me. (I liked catching the big frog in the pond as a kid.) This principle will help us when we get to the actual planning, but for now it is begging the question, "How do you find the biggest frog?"

Think about your time like money. Let's say your job or your time is worth $25 per hour. Work out your daily calendar and decide how much time each thing that you do takes. Then multiply it by $25 to determine the values of each task. One of the things I do is online shop—to death. I research the price and the model ad nauseam and finally, after finding the best price, I purchase it and give myself a gold star. The problem is that the hour or two (okay, four or five) that I took just cost me $50. I saved $10 on the purchase. That is not a good plan.

Your life—your time, which is your most valuable resource—must be mastered. Running around like a chicken with your head cut off crying out for more hours in the day is not how you want to live your life. No matter where you are in life, you can no longer afford to live that way. You must live purposefully. In order to make a change in any of the six areas of life, you have to plan that change and its implementation: ruling our time instead of being ruled by time. You know you are ruled by time when you say, "I just wish I had more hours in the day." (I think I just stepped on everybody's toes including mine.) It is our inability to settle the fact that there are only 24 hours in every day and 7 days in every week. When we find ourselves wanting to change that fact, we become a slave to time. May I suggest that we all start thanking God for our time, all 24 hours of it, and approach the day glad to have every hour to be utilized to the highest degree, even the hours of sleep, rest and entertainment. You want to take control of your minutes, hours, days, months, years and so on. Even if you are more of a fly-by-the-seat-of-your-pants type of person, or a person who is super kick-back, you have got to admit that you would like to get a few more things done in the day, even if it is to have more relaxation time.

To do that you can't be a victim to time, you have to be its master. For example:

- A victim says they just didn't have enough time to get to that. A master plans when they will get to that.
- A victim is always late with an excuse or external circumstance. A master plans well and is on time.
- A victim says everything takes too long. A master thinks that things will take a certain amount of time, and if it does take longer than expected, he/she rearranges their schedule to accommodate the extra time that task will take.
- A victim has an excuse for everything they don't get done. A master admits it was his/her fault and goes back to find out what the problem was and corrects it.

We were created with mastery in mind. It is our very design to master time or God wouldn't have told Adam and Eve to manage the earth. That was a big task, but God thought they were up to it because He created them to be able. This is true of you too. You are up to the task, although as we go through this process, you may need to dump some tasks.

Scheduling, or time management, is a tool or a means to get you to your end goal. It is a thoughtful, purposeful approach to achieving what you want to achieve. It is like your job. Hopefully, your job is not your end goal. You job or career is a means to an end. We don't live to work; we work to live. My job allows me to make money in order to feed and care for my family among other things. It so happens that I have a few jobs that coincide with my mission in life, which is nice, however it can be harmful as well. Let's face it: none of us, if we had a week to live, would work a 60-hour work week. Why? Because that is not the goal of our life. It is not our mission. For most, it is a means to an end, and for some it has a calling attached to it. Yet even those like myself with a calling would not spend much, if any, time working.

Probably zero hours if I have seven days to live. Face it: your work is not on your bucket list. Time management is a tool to keep work and everything else in proper missional perspective.

Before we get into mission and the process of creating a life plan, I have a scary assignment. For two weeks, if you dare, write down everything you do and the time it takes to do it. When I used the word everything, I meant everything. You can use an app, or software, or a piece of paper, just write it all down. You will probably weed some things out just because you are recording it, but that is okay. What you want to see is pattern and time wasters. You will find them. You will see many things that you haven't noticed. I must warn you that you will be tempted to cheat to make yourself look good. Resist the temptation. Ask God to help you be honest with yourself. Get a hold of what you are doing and most of you will see that you have more time than you think to get more things done, or to just relax and read a magazine.

Mission

If I asked you what the top two things are that you do, and I gave you 30 seconds to answer, what would the answers be? If I asked you this question when you were on your deathbed, what would you look back and think was the most important thing you did? If you asked God what the top three things you were made for are, what do you think they would they be? The first thing to any type of plan, whether it is a business plan or a life plan, is to find your mission. Your mission is purpose in life. Your mission isn't about who you are as much as it is where you are going. For instance, two of my missions in life are to be a great husband and great father. Those are missions. We all have several missions that will guide our lives if we take the time to articulate them in writing.

The book of Proverbs says that where there is no vision, no revelation, no seeing into the future, the people cast off restraint (Proverbs 29:18). In other words, they run amuck when there is no finish line that is outlined. We all need to articulate our mission. Why are you here? What is the most important outcome of your life? What about the second most important? What defines a successful mission? Unlike *Mission: Impossible* (the old one with Peter Graves)[9] it isn't an episode long with another mission coming next week. A mission is lifelong, or at least decades long most of the time. If your mission is to be rich (I'm not convinced that is a good mission), then do you want to be rich for 20 years, or your whole life long? You get the point.

Things that fit within your mission are your top priorities. Even fitness can earn a spot on the schedule if you want to be healthy, but it must be put in priority according to your mission and not according to your desired six-pack abs. Ray Johnson, in his book *CEO Logic: Hot to Think and Act like a Chief Executive*, writes, "Prioritizing is the answer to time management problems—not computers, efficiency experts, or matrix scheduling. You do not need to do work faster or to eliminate gaps in productivity to make better use of your time. You need to spend more time on the right things..."[10]

One incredibly helpful thing that I do every year, is take a one to three night getaway to work on my assignments for the coming year. My mission stays the same, but my assignment on how to accomplish that mission often changes. Priorities change too. I schedule according to my priorities. So I have to set them and I do that on a solo getaway. For me, it is my trailer at the beach. I connect with God very well at the beach, and for me, this time is not spent in reflection so much as it is getting my marching orders from God. I come back with my schedule in the computer and I am ready to tackle the year. I have mission objectives, priority "hats," time plans including family vacations and getaways with my wife (that should be reason enough to send your husbands ladies), and a real sense of direction and purpose. However, you can do this in a few afternoons if that is not feasible. I think it is preferable.

Step 1

Write down all the things you do. All the hats you wear. If you are a working mother, you have more hats than a clown's dressing room. Write them all down. If you are your gardener, write it down as well as if you fix your own cars. Don't leave anything out. Whatever you are responsible to do, write it down.

Step 2

Go back and answer the questions I just asked you about mission, what is your purpose? What is the most important outcome in your life? Write down the answers to those questions and then begin to enlarge your thinking to incorporate all that your mission(s) may include. Your mission must be written and clearly defined and understood. This may take some time, so set some time aside to work on it. The favorable outcome of your life depends on it. Another question that may be helpful is: where do you want to be in 20 years? Not how much wealth you have or where you live, but what do you want your life to look like? If you could name three 20-year goals, what would they be?

Step 3

Looking at the list above, circle the top three priorities. After you do that, number their priority according to your mission. If they don't line up with your mission, start a new list and circle the top three again, then prioritize them. Go through the list and put an X next to anything that doesn't fall in with your mission. You are not getting rid of them, just identifying them. Next go through the list again and cross off the things that you don't have to do. These are things that someone else could do.

Those top three things are special. This is where the 80/20 principle comes in which says that 80 percent of your goals can be accomplished by working on 20 percent of your tasks. Those top two or three things are where your time and energy need to go. This goes for your daily lists of to-do's as well. Look at your top three again and see how they will accomplish more than your numbers four through six.

Step 4

Make a fresh list in order of priority of everything that is left—with the X hats at the bottom, of course. This is the list that you will now use to create your life schedule. A life schedule is a weekly and possibly a monthly living template. You will create your daily schedules from this template with few exceptions. It is very important to whittle down your list. You can't have 17 different things you do on your schedule if you work full time. Try to get rid of as much as possible before you write this list.

Step 5

Create the calendar, your life template if you will. This will take some time, thought, prayer, and a tall glass or cup of your favorite beverage. This is going to take incredible concentration. Plot out your life. Start with the big things that just can't change first, such as sleep and work. Block those out. Planning your bedtime may seem like you are sending yourself to your room, but if you are a busy person, then you need to plan your sleep as well as everything else in your schedule.

After the non-negotiable, everything should be scheduled according to priority. Top priorities get the first shot at the time slots they need. After you have fit (or haven't fit) everything in, go back and rework it. I like doing this in MS Excel so I can color code things, which makes them stand out to me, but you can do it however you want. In fact, everyone is unique so you have to plan your schedule the way it will work for you, but don't use that as an excuse not to plan. Fill out your life template. Very few things get done on accident (although I had seven children on accident, only one was planned). You can do this!

Now go over your schedule one last time. Did you add in any free time or flex time? If not, go back and rework it. To have no flex time is to set yourself up for perfectionism, frustration or failure. You need some flex time. You can use it to produce or you can use it to relax. Maybe you can use it to read a book or magazine or whatever. Just put it in your schedule. You will thank me later.

You are done! Now you get to walk it out.

Weekly, Daily and To-Do's

After your life plan is done and you are confident that you will be moving towards your mission (or missions) in life, you are ready to book your week up. As I said before, I fill in all the important yearly things first. Things need to move for your kid's birthday or anniversary or Christmas. Those are abnormal days just like vacation days. They have their own rule or principle. Get 'er done!

Weekly

So you have your weekly planner in front of you and now you fill in your weekly, honest to goodness calendar. This is not a template, this is what you will do the week of September 2, or whenever. When things come up that don't have a slot, you are going to have to make a choice and sometimes that choice is going to be, "I'm sorry, I won't be able to do that." Say it out loud. Now call someone close to you and say it. They won't understand why you are saying it, but I just want you to practice. While you have them on the phone, practice this: "Hey, could you do [fill in the blank] for me?" That is called delegation and that has to be a missile in your arsenal. You are too focused on your mission to get distracted doing things that other people could do. Again, they won't know why you are asking them to give your dog a bath, but you never know, they may say yes. You have to weed out and delegate those things that don't belong on your weekly or daily schedule. So have a place to write those things down, because I know these items still need to be accomplished, it's just that you aren't going to do them. Some would say it takes too long if someone else does it, and I can do it better and faster anyway. I know. I agree. Delegate it or dump it. It can't fit on your very important schedule.

Daily

Every day you are going to look at your schedule for the day, or the night before, and decide what needs fine-tuning. Hopefully your day is more open than expected and you can concentrate on the report, the upcoming project, the gift for your wife, or whatever else is coming up. Working ahead? Oh, what a feeling. You will reduce stress, which will make you healthier and happier, which will make you a better spouse and parent, which will surely fulfill one of your missions.

To-do's

Everyone needs a to-do list. It is a way to mentally dump all those things you are trying to remember to do. At the beginning of every week, go through your to-do list and (guess what I am going to say) dump or delegate what you can. The rest of the items get prioritized based on importance and urgency. Get the big ones out of the way first. Assign the remaining to-do items to your weekly schedule. Caution! You may run out of time. You may have too many to-do items and they won't all fit in your calendar. Then they don't get done. You are only one person, and you can't do it all. So settle with the fact that you only have so many working hours in a day. You get to choose what things get done and what things are left for another day.

This is where the daily schedule comes in. It is such a freeing thing to be able to see that you can't do it all instead of at the end of the day you are so upset because you couldn't get it all done. Schedule your day hour by hour at the very least and be realistic with the time you give projects. Have I said to include some flex time? With a pressing deadline or a busy season, you will want to cut your rest down and get rid of your flex time, or cancel your date night with your spouse or your night out with friends. Don't do it. Stick to your plan. Don't let your emotions decide. You had a plan at the beginning of the year and at the beginning of the month, week and day. So stick to it.

Final Encouragement

Remember, all this stuff has to be written or typed out so you can see it. Planning your life is seeing your plan. One thing that I have found to be helpful is to work backwards from an appointment. I always think that I can squeeze one more thing in, but if I have an appointment at 12:00, and it takes 20 minutes to get there, 30 minutes to plan for it and 10 minutes to gather the material needed for it, then the start time for the meeting prep is 11:00. If I am smart, I will build in 15-20 minutes for the unexpected, especially if it is an important meeting. So work backwards and set your alarm to go off.

Review and evaluate yesterday and last week. How did you do? What adjustments need to be made? Do you see a pattern? Do you need more flex time? Are you trying to do too much? Are there too many to-do items left without remedy? Your schedule will change and be fine-tuned all the time. That's alright. You can do this. You are scheduling your next level of living in certain areas. You are making changes. You are planning for these changes and giving them time to happen because you know that if you don't plan it, it probably won't happen. You understand that climbing the staircase to the next level takes effort, but rolling down the stairs just takes gravity. Climbing. One step at a time. Be patient. Be resolute. You got this.

13

The Truth About You – and God

God is asking all of us if we will believe what He promised to us. He is asking us to contend for the vision that He gave us. Where do you think all of your hopes and dreams come from? Some of you haven't allowed yourselves to go there in quite some time. Will you go there again? Will you tell yourself that it will just have to submit to your higher call, your destiny?

Jesus came to bring salvation, liberty, healing, wisdom and understanding of who God is and how much He loves us; and to gain victory over all of the destructive things in us. God wants our relationships, our marriages, and our friendships to be great. He is glorified in your great marriage. I am not sure how your mediocre marriage can bring glory to God. Jesus came to bring us life and to have it to the full. Can you begin to believe that?

The realization of God's epic plan for you will only come through knowing God's incredible power and love towards you, and knowing His astounding will for your life. You need to understand that His power that is in you will empower you to make choice after choice to believe and to discipline yourself to live like you believe. The question is, do you believe what God said is true?

He says: *I like you. You are special. You are a treasure to me. You are worth it. You have great meaning. I delight in you. There is greatness in*

179

you. You have what it takes. You will always be loved. You are significant. I challenge you to wake up and look into the mirror every morning and recite some of those things that come right out of the Bible. Yes, He knows your weaknesses, and it doesn't change a thing. In fact, it is His specialty to use weak vessels for great exploits.

Jacob was a cheater. Moses was a stutterer. David had an affair. Noah got drunk and naked. Rehab and Mary Magdalene were prostitutes. Paul was a murderer. Jonah ran from God. Martha was a worrier. Gideon was insecure. Miriam was a gossip. Elijah was moody. Thomas was a doubter. Sarah was impatient and laughed at God. Zacchaeus was short. Jeremiah was young. Abraham was old, and Lazarus was dead. What is your excuse now?

There is a story about a woman who has to go walk quite a distance to get water. She had jugs to carry the water in, but one of them had a small crack. After quite some time and many trips to the river for water, the cracked pot spoke up and told the woman that he should be thrown away because he was cracked. "By the time you get back home," the pot said, "I am only half full." The woman answered the pot and said, "I knew you were cracked so I planted seeds along the road. Every time I came back from the river you would water the seeds and they grew to become the flowers that I pick and put on my kitchen table. Because of you, I always have beautiful flowers in my home." God isn't looking for perfection; he wants you to be you.

Genetic Maximum

We have built-in potential that most of us never reach. Some don't even believe they could get there if they wanted to. Yet that potential still exists for you. Our God-given potential is untapped by many for various reasons, yet God doesn't take it away from us. It is still there. Some of it is locked up in your DNA. It is in our design. It is our God created potential. For many their potential is hidden away in the vault of mediocre. It's like an A student getting B's and C's instead. The potential is there but it takes effort to attain. First, it takes believing. You won't spend the energy for something that you don't believe is possible. It is time to start believing that you are created for greatness and not to be mediocre, no matter what kind of cracks are in your pot.

Graveyards are filled with unrealized dreams and untapped talents. They are filled with people who, for one reason or another, took what they had to offer in this life to their graves. We have a maximum potential beyond what we think. The way we think and the way we live will determine whether we go to the grave with our potential untapped and with our dreams unrealized. You may think that you don't have much to do with your future. What can you do? It's too late, you are too old, or you are too broken. Or you are too young or too heavy, too skinny or too... the list goes on. I am here to tell you that you have what it takes!

There is this concept that we have about turning 40. When I had my 40th birthday party, my friends and family really went all out. They blindfolded me and dressed me in old guy clothes. Then they hung a sign around me saying, "Say hi to the old fart—he turned 40 today." Then they paraded me blindfolded around downtown Huntington Beach. People kept saying, "Hey you old fart," and I didn't get why until I was un-blindfolded. Then I went to a party where everyone wore black and all the decorations were in black. I got a walker with a surfboard rack on top of it for gosh sakes! Do you know what they called that party? An "over the hill" party. It was all fun and games and honestly I did enjoy myself and my wife got retribution for all of the practical jokes I have played on her over the years. Yet, there is this concept, over the hill. Where did that come from? Who made that up? At 40 I was smarter, wiser, richer, more successful, more happily married, kinder and less abrasive, and a dozen other things than when I was 21. What hill are they talking about? At 21 I did stupid stuff regularly, and at 40, well, I still do stupid stuff, but not so often. Are you with me? I have grown and progressed. I am the improved model in nearly every way.

How about physically? That is what the hill is about, right? It is half way through your life. Even if I accept that as truth, which I don't, who says I am going downhill? Listen carefully—if we think and believe with our heart that we will go downhill, we most likely will go downhill. Downhill means you are going to degrade and degenerate. Although there is some truth to that on a cellular level, the minute we accept that as absolute truth, we fix a sentence on ourselves. That is not good. Moses died at 120, as did Joshua. I don't have any plans to live that long, but listen to what was said about them when they died.

They were full of strength. Did you get that? That tells me that I am nowhere near the downside of whatever hill they are talking about. I like to look at the later third of life as a steeper grade. First of all, I am not coasting. That is for sure. It takes more effort to stay in shape than it did when I was in my twenties. Secondly, I am not declining. I am continuing to climb and will continue to do so until God calls me home or my parachute doesn't open. I am not Jack LaLanne, but I would like to be fit like him well into my 80s and 90s. What I am saying is that none of us have to accept the over the hill concept; we just have to work smarter and harder. Lucky for us, we know how to do that because of our years on this earth. The youth is truly wasted on the young.

Let me give you a couple of examples of the impact you can have on your own lifespan:

> *The fear of the Lord adds length to life, but the years of the wicked are cut short.* (Proverbs 10:27) *[11]For through wisdom your days will be many, and years will be added to your life. [12]If you are wise, your wisdom will reward you; if you are a mocker, you alone will suffer.* (Proverbs 9:11–12)

> *[1]My son, do not forget my teaching, but keep my commands in your heart, [2]for they will prolong your life many years and bring you prosperity.* (Proverbs 3:1–2)

You have a say in how old you get! Imagine that. You also can help your longevity through proper nutrition and eating, fitness and overall health principles, like proper sleep. Tack onto that the wonderful advances in our knowledge of the brain and the impact our very own thoughts have on our longevity and we really do have a recipe for a great later third of life. These things not only add length to your life, but they add quality to your days. You have impact. The choices you make throughout your life have impact. Even those negative things have impact, but the beautiful thing is that our bodies have such wonderful potential to right the wrongs. It isn't instant and there are things that are difficult to reverse, but there is so much that can be done. Then you factor in God and His incredible love for us, His incredible supernatural power, and you have hope again. There is hope!

Prayer works. There have been some major studies about the effectiveness of prayer. All that I have seen are coming back with this theory: prayer makes things better. It may be that people are comforted or encouraged by it, which helps tremendously because it augments our thinking, which is a key. Yet there is something beyond that, something in the unseen realm. It is the intervention of a gracious God. Prayer changes things. Ask Jabez. He prayed this quick little prayer: "'Oh, that you would bless me and enlarge my territory! Let your hand be with me, and keep me from harm so that I will be free from pain.' And God granted his request." (1 Chronicles 4:10) Jabez means pain. He was named in a time when names meant something about a person. His was pain. Bummer. Every time he heard his name, he heard, "you are a pain." He wanted to change the course of His life, so He prayed. It happened.

Think about it like this. God loves to bring awe and wonder. He loves when His creation looks at stuff and says, "Wow, that is awesome." When you live a mediocre life, is anyone going to say that about you? There are no awards for mediocre. Jesus prayed in John 17 that we would have His glory. His plan is to share it with us. Is that incredible to you? It is true. His glory in us brings Him glory, which will bring mankind back to God. Your part to play matters. Your life is for more than you. It has more meaning than your family. Your significance is great! That is why this stuff matters so much. That is why God wants your life to flourish in every area.

Amber Corson was a stay-at-home mom with three young children. When her husband was laid off from his Florida construction job as the economy soured, Amber had to take a night-shift job to help support the family.

She'd been working that late shift for four weeks. One night she was driving home, tired, scared, missing her kids, and worried about their future. Amber felt like God had bigger plans for her family than to struggle. She prayed on that drive home. "God, please tell me what I can do to get my family through this." She said His response came to her "like a breath."

"I gave you a gift. Go plant gardens. Do your heart's work."

Amber had a degree in horticulture that she'd never used. She was so talented she'd been certified as a master gardener. She had a natural talent for making things grow. That night, she told her husband what God had put in her heart. She prayed on it. In the next few weeks, she said, "Things just fell into place like it had been planned for me all along."

She called her landscaping business Eden Paradise Gardens. It grew quickly and flourished beyond anything she had dreamed. It was her time!

God wants to breathe new life into your dreams.[1]

Don't be one who is hindered by what you think is possible. When we understand the power that God has already given to us, and His might that He freely gives to us, we can't be stopped. I know that some of you reading this book are going through tough times. You are in the middle of a terrible situation. Keep going! You will make it out the other side. Ask a woman what the most painful part of the pregnancy is and she will say the delivery. Ask her what part of the delivery is the most painful part and she will tell you it is right before the baby is born. I think it is that way in life sometimes. Right before we are about to get our breakthrough, our promotion, a restored relationship, it gets really tough. Hard times are a part of life. You determine whether they will break you or they will make you.

God Spoke to Us in His Word

[20]*Now to him who is able to do immeasurably more than all we ask or imagine, according to his power that is at work within us,* [21]*to him be glory in the church and in Christ Jesus throughout all generations, for ever and ever! Amen.* (Ephesians 3:20–21)

Did you get that? More than you could ask for. Immeasurably more than you could imagine. I can imagine a lot. According to His ability (power) at work in us—God's ability is at work in you! You have success in your future. Don't give up and don't give in. If you're going through hell, keep going and get through it. Don't give up and sit down at a rest stop in hell.

Today is the day!

Down in the Florida Keys, there was a treasure hunter whose motto was "Today's the day." Every day for sixteen years, Mel Fisher sent his divers out with those encouraging words to find a Spanish ship that sank off the Keys in 1622. He often had to pay his men in promises while dodging bill collectors. He and his family lived on a leaky houseboat for years. One of his sons and a daughter-in-law were lost at sea as they searched for the treasure.

Still, Fisher never gave up. He refused to abandon his dream or to give in to critics and doubters. He held on by declaring that each day would be the day. Then, in 1985, Mel's divers found the "mother lode" of gold and silver and jewelry from the wreckage of the Spanish galleon. Nearly thirty years later, divers were still bringing up treasure from that site.

Is today the day for you to accomplish your goal, to land your dream job, to find love, to restore your health?[2]

It is time to start speaking out our right thinking. My memory is improving. I am beginning to stress less about everything. I am getting in shape. I have an outrageously good marriage. I have more than enough financially. I am a great student well able to excel in every class. I can stay pure and walk strong with God. My relationship with my children will be restored. I will live in health. I will get out of debt. I will sleep well. The list could go on. Pick some things and say them out loud. Let yourself hear them.

If God has declared something to us, then it will happen. When He says it, He commits Himself and all of His resources to bringing it about. That is a lot of resource! So stop telling yourself why you can't and start telling yourself that you are a champion. Greatness is in you and you are about to elevate to the next level in every area of life.

14

This Never Stops – Keep Climbing

If you have made it this far in this book then your life has already begun to change. You may not have applied anything thus far, but you have learned and thought about it. That is the beginning. If you have read it slowly, you have thought about it a lot. You will never be the same. Part of the reason is that you know what you now know and you have the seed of promise rising in you to abundance in every area of life. It is easier to believe for some areas more than others, but you are stirred. How do I know? Well, it is not because I am such a great writer. It is because your mind has been processing for hours and the seeds of greatness that are in you are at least beginning to germinate if they haven't already sprouted in a way that you have never seen before. By finishing the book you have proven that you are a finisher. A mediocre person would have stopped in Chapter 3 or maybe 4, but not you!

If you have begun to implement some changes then you have already attained your next level. The fact that you moved it from knowledge to practice means that you are not settling for mediocrity. You are on your way to elevating your way of living. Your culture shift is right around the corner. In fact, it is right in front of you. You have decided to reach for more, for your own sake, for the sake of your family and friends, and for those lives that you will touch. You have decided to go towards your destiny that God has apportioned you. You are honoring Him by reaching higher. Welcome to the journey towards extraordinary.

The next level mentality has grabbed you. It is kind of exciting to think that you will be better off next year than you are this year, isn't it? Most people want to be better off, but when you believe you *will be* better off, you have turned the corner. You have entered the highway upon which those who are successful travel. You will be named with all those who allowed God's incredible destiny to take hold of them— those people who changed and became someone great.

This is a life-long journey. You don't just fill out a worksheet, concentrate for 21 days to see the change and then quit. No way! You keep going. You have momentum on your side and there is something to momentum. Don't squander it. Don't be like those who win their first race and then retire. That's like passing a class and not getting your degree, or inventing a successful product and never inventing again. You must take every milestone and use that as a springboard to your next one.

You have decided to deny mediocrity, which is wonderful! Don't embrace perfectionism, which will ultimately kill you! Perfectionism is a trap designed to ensnare you. What happens when you step into a bear trap or any other trap? You are not going to go any further. It reminds me of movies like *Swiss Family Robinson*[1] or *Indiana Jones* where a trap would be set so when a guy triggers the trap by stepping into the noose on the ground he ends up hanging upside down from the tree.[2] That is what perfectionism is like. It stops your progress and all the blood rushes to your head until you explode. Even if you are moving forward in, let's say…finances, you will be suffering in your mental, physical, emotional, and relational areas if you are striving at perfectionism. It is a killer because it is a mentality that will ultimately rule you. Now you are enslaved all over again. This mentality comes from believing that you *have to be* perfect to *be* anything worthwhile. Everybody has this little box that they fill in. The box is the answer to this question: "I am worthwhile if…" Or, "I am worthwhile when…" This may be a little too simplistic, but perfectionism comes from the belief system that I am worthwhile if I am perfect, or near perfect. Most perfectionists wouldn't even admit to that, but they truly believe it. It is a trap! What is the "perfect" thing to have in the box? God loves me. That never changes. Therefore, my personhood, my worth is based on God's opinion of me and not others nor my own.

If you have learned anything thus far, you have learned that you are not interested in being perfect (or making others perfect); you are interested in being the best possible you. The last time I checked, your best wasn't perfect all the time. Without relaxing your desire to be great, allow failures and hiccups. Do I have to go back to the Thomas Edison story again? He didn't consider his attempts as failures, just ways his inventions didn't work. Cut yourself some slack if you tend towards this performance mentality. Correct your thinking. You know how to do that!

Make a decision right now that you won't be stopped—you can't be stopped. If you need to, go back and re-read the Torpedoes That Can Sink You chapter and determine that you are going to be torpedo proof. There has to be grit in your soul that is going to be tough to go against. Plus you are enjoying it, right? We have to enjoy the journey. We can't look at this like some kind of performance we have to get right and we are going to grit our teeth and bare it, do what is right, be better if it kills us, and hang on with white knuckles until we get to the finish line. Laugh a little. In fact, laugh a lot. Remember it is healthy for your body and your brain. Some of this will be tough and it will take discipline, but if it is always all business all the time, struggling and grunting, and you can't enjoy the smell of the flowers, you have missed the point. Life is meant to be enjoyed. Can you imagine a good father not wanting his kids to enjoy their lives? He knows there will be times of intense studying, exhausting practices, difficult rejections and hard work, but he wants them to enjoy the overall experience of living. God is no different. He has designed life to be enjoyed. So much of the suffering we see and read about is because humans went haywire. Yes, there are tough times for everybody in the best of circumstances, but those tough times will build us into the strong, wise and capable people to which we aspire. So have some fun, laugh at yourself when you fall short, and get up and get going again.

When you prevail, when you have a breakthrough, when you hit your next level, do a touchdown dance. Celebrate the victories, those things that are to be celebrated. Don't let them pass you by without a dance. I got a call for my first major speaking engagement. I would speak to several thousand pastors and leaders about physical health. I got off the phone and you would have thought Ochocinco (a football player known for his touchdown dances) just entered the room. This engagement was all God's doing, and it deserved a celebration. Whether it is spending time consistently with God for a month, or losing 15 pounds, or realizing your stress level has dropped, or your spouse told you that you are a great husband (or wife) and they could tell that you have been putting in the effort to be great, or whatever— celebrate!

When I first bought my Galaxy SIII (a cellphone) I asked Skyvi (an automated assistant), "What is my purpose?" Her answer was, "Hopefully we are all doing God's work." If an Android app can get this right, so can we. If all that we do is only for us to be personally satisfied, we will end up on the short end of the stick. We are fulfilling God's purpose by living His design for our lives. His design for our lives is to be significant contributors in the lives of others. We are bringing glory to God when we continue to grow into our destiny. When we are living and exposing the greatness that He put in us, we bring a smile to His face and encouragement to others. Let's live for something much more than ourselves.

Take someone with you on the journey. Pour yourself into someone else. Help them get to their next level. Whether it is praying for them, giving them some lessons you have learned along the way, being their workout buddy or just being their cheerleader, give away what you have received. One of the keys to the Kingdom of God is to give and you will be kept full. So find somebody and help them on their journey. You have something to give, you. There is someone out there, many out there, that will hear you (because you are you) when they wouldn't hear anybody else. There are people that just need someone to believe in them. They need someone to call them higher and to tell them that they can do it. They have never heard it. Be that person. Pour your life into others and be part of their story of greatness.

Finally, please send me a letter or email of your story (totallifepursuit@gmail.com). I would love to hear it. Listening to people overcoming and breaking through, or just deciding to begin the journey out of mediocre-land brings joy and encouragement to me.

15

Invitation

Throughout this book I have spoken of God as if I somehow know Him. I do. My whole life I have felt like He was calling me to something. As a little tike of 5 years old, I would ask my mom to take me to church. I don't know why. She took me, or rather dropped me off and I went. Fast forward to summer camp 1975, I gave my life to Christ. I haven't always been the greatest example of someone who calls himself a Christian, but I tried to serve God. Then it happened. I got a revelation of what God really wanted. He wanted me to apprehend the love He has for me. I was, as you are, created for relationship with God. We are created to experience and know His love in the deepest way. That is the thing that filled my voids and it will fill yours too. The revelation I got right beside that was that my job was to love Him. I thought that I had to do this and stop doing that, but it wasn't about *doing*, it was about *being*—being loved, being his adopted son so to speak. Everything flows from relationship with God and not what we do for God. Giving my life to Christ is the most important and best decision of my life. The second is marrying my wife of nearly 28 years, Lora. There is a third. It was to let God love me and to let my life be lived out of love for Him. Knowing that when I die I will be with God is superb, but even that flows from the fact that He loves me and I decided to accept that love, that relationship, and love Him in return.

If you have never accepted that love or accepted the offer from God of relationship, I would like to help you do so through a simple prayer (prayer is talking to God). There is something you should know—you will never be the same. Life won't get easier necessarily, but it will have more meaning for sure. You will know and experience the love that I am talking about as well as be able to stand on every promise that God has made, including heaven. There is one catch. To have His life, you must give yours up. That is the way of the Kingdom. Giving your life up means that you don't get to rule it anymore. Yet you aren't lost in the transaction. In fact, the real you will begin to emerge. When you make Jesus your Lord, you make Him your decision maker. It's a great deal. You give him your life and He gives you His forgiveness, removes your shame, gives you His love and gives you the full rights of sonship. I encourage you to pray with me.

Father, I want you to be my father and I want to be your son (daughter). I am ready to give my life to you and let you be my decision maker. Please forgive me for everything I have ever done to offend you and cleanse me from the muck I have brought into my own life. I want to know your love and experience it. I want to love you back. Teach me how to love. Thank you for sending your son to make this all possible. Amen.

There is another person I want to invite to pray as well. It is the person who has made some kind of commitment to Christ, but you haven't lived in His love. In fact, your life has been lived for yourself. Whether you have been immoral or just been practicing religion, it is time for you to come home to Papa. His arms are open to you, so stop your works, whatever they are, and rest in His love and enjoy relationship with Him. It will take repentance (a change of mind) and a change of mindset. I encourage you to pray with me.

Father, I don't know where I got off track, but I am coming back to you. I will make my life about receiving your love and loving you in return. Forgive me, Papa. Cleanse me. Restore me. I need your arms around me. Help me to think differently, to truly change my mindset. Free me from those things that kept me away from you. Thank you. Amen.

Acknowledgements

Undertaking this project has been long and hard. Most things that are worth something take that kind of effort. There have been many people who have helped me and encouraged me along the way. Thank you Spencer and Jeremy for helping me get this project off the ground. Without you I wouldn't have a title let alone a beginning. Thank you Sean for all your support and wisdom and if I can speak in faith, your continued support and wisdom. Thank you to Alicia and Karen for helping with the editing of this project. There are no words that would come close to thanking Ashley Afable for her valuable help, guidance, editing, design, ideas and encouragement. You are a great editor and cheerleader! Thank you Hope Chapel OC church family for allowing me the time to complete this project and a special thanks to the Miller Tribe. You are the bomb! To my wife, Lora, my honey-baby, my lover who has listened to me talk about this for hours and has shipped me off to write alone, you are the best. I am and will always be head over heels in love with you.

I thought about if I should thank God first or last. I chose last so it would linger with whoever reads this. God is my source, my everything, the one who gives me life, joy, health, peace, and every other thing that is good. Papa, you gave me the inspiration, the ideas and the strength and wisdom to write this book and birth a ministry that will help tens of thousands and I pray millions. Thank you for letting me be a part of something that is so much bigger than me.

Notes

Chapter 6: Physical Part of the Whole

1. Micheal A. Clark, Brian G. Sutton and Scott C. Lucett, *NASM Essentials of Personal Fitness Training*, 4th edition, (Baltimore: Lippincott Williams & Wilkins, 2011).
2. Chris Crowley and Henry S. Lodge M.D., *Younger Next Year: Live Strong, Fit, and Sexy—Until You're 80 And Beyond*, Kindle edition, (New York: Workman Publishing Company, Inc., 2007), 8.
3. Ibid, 64-67.
4. *You Asked for It*, Television series, DuMont Television Network, 1950.
5. Chris Crowley and Henry S. Lodge M.D., *Younger Next Year: Live Strong, Fit, and Sexy—Until You're 80 And Beyond*, Kindle edition, (New York: Workman Publishing Company, Inc., 2007), 71.
6. Brian Tracy, Eat *That Frog!: 21 Great Ways To Stop Procrastinating And Get More Done In Less Time*, 2nd edition, (San Francisco: Berrett-Koehler Publishers, 2007).

Chapter 7: Mental Part of the Whole

1. David R. Hamilton, PhD, "Do Positive People Live Longer?" Huffpost - Healthy Living, November 2, 2010, http://www.huffingtonpost.com/david-r-hamilton-phd/positive-people-live-long_b_774648.html
2. Dawson Church, The Genie in Your Genes: Epigenetic Medicine

and the New Biology of Intention, (Santa Rosa, CA. Energy Psychology Press, 2008).

3. Dr. Caroline Leaf, blog article, "You Are What You Think," Dr. Leaf's personal website Switch On Your Brain, November 30, 2011, http://drleaf.com/blog/general/you-are-what-you-think-75-98-of-mental-and-physical-illnesses-come-from-our-thought-life, accessed October 5, 2013.

4. Glen Rein, PhD, and Rollin McCraty, PhD, "Local and Non-Local Effects of Coherent Heart Frequencies on Conformational Changes of DNA," Institute of HeartMath, January 1, 2011, http://appreciativeinquiry.case.edu/practice/organizationDetail.cfm?coid=852&sector=32, accessed October 5, 2013.

5. Merriam-Webster, online ed., s.v. "Mind," http://www.merriam-webster.com/dictionary/mind.

6. Tom Geoghegan, "Who, What, Why: How Long is the Ideal Nap?" BBC News, Washington DC, April 28, 2011, http://www.bbc.co.uk/news/world-us-canada-13232034.

7. Dr. Caroline Leaf, The Gift In You: Discovering New Life Through Gifts Hidden In Your Mind, Kindle edition, (Nashville, TN: Thomas Nelson, Inc., 2009), 482-484.

8. Ibid.

9. Brian Tracy, Eat That Frog!: 21 Great Ways To Stop Procrastinating And Get More Done In Less Time, 2nd edition, (San Francisco: Berrett-Koehler Publishers, 2007).

Chapter 8: Emotional Part of the Whole

1. Wikipedia, "Cortisol," http://en.wikipedia.org/wiki/Cortisol#cite_note-isbn0-87893-620-3-46 (accessed October 5, 2013).

2. Elissa S. Epel, PhD, Bruce McEwen, PhD, Teresa Seeman, PhD, Karen Matthews, PhD, Grace Castellazzo, RN, BSN, Kelly D. Brownell, PhD, Jennifer Bell, BA and Jeannette R. Ickovics, PhD, "Stress and Body Shape: Stress-Induced Cortisol Secretion is Consistently Greater Among Women with Central Fat," Psychosomatic Medicine, vol. 62, no. 5 (2000): 623-632,

http://www.psychosomaticmedicine.org/content/62/
5/623.long. Quoted in The Cortisol Connection, "Cortisol, stress
and abdominal fat," 2012, http://cortisol.com/cortisol-stress-
abdominal-fat.

3. Denise Reynolds, "Stress, Cortisol, and Weight Gain: Hormonal
    Response Can Cause Weight Loss Failure," Suite101.com
    (Vancouver, Canada), August 26, 2009,
    http://suite101.com/a/stress-cortisol-and-weight-gain-a142833.
    Quoted in Commit To Be Fit, "Cortisol Series – 1 of 7: Cortisol,
    Stress and Your Weight," April 5, 2013,
    http://commit2bfit.me/cortisol-series-1-of-7-cortisol-stress-
    your-weight.

4. John R. Lee, M.D. and Virginia Hopkins, "Cortisol and the Stress
    Connection: Balanced Cortisol Levels are Essential to Optimal
    Health," Virginia Hopkins Health Watch,
    http://www.virginiahopkinstestkits.com/cortisolstress.html
    (accessed October 5, 2013). Quoted in The Cortisol
    Connection, online article, "The Cortisol-Stress Connection,"
    2012, http://cortisol.com/the-cortisol-stress-connection.

5. Aeron Biotechnology, Aeron Biotechnology Lifecycles Clinical
    Laboratory, http://www.aeron.com. Quoted in The Cortisol
    Connection, online article, "The Cortisol-Stress Connection,"
    2012, http://cortisol.com/the-cortisol-stress-connection.

6. Wendell C. Sleet, Scaleless Dieting: The Essential Survival Kit
    For The Overweight, Obese And Diabetics, eBook,
    (Bloomington, IN: AuthorHouseTM, 2011), 89,
    http://books.google.com/books?id=zpVLHNNQk40C&printse
    c=copyright#v=onepage&q&f=false.

7. Dr. Caroline Leaf, Who Switched Off My Brain? Controlling
    Toxic Thoughts and Emotions, rev. ed. (Nashville, TN: Thomas
    Nelson Publishers, 2009).

8. Randy J. Nelson, An Introduction To Behavioral Endocrinology,
    4th ed., (Sunderland, MA: Sinauer Associates Inc., 2011) quoted
    in Wikipedia, "Cortisol" 2013.

9. Don Colbert M.D., Deadly Emotions: Understand the Mind-
    Body-Spirit Connection That Can Heal or Destroy You,
    (Nashville, TN: Thomas Nelson, Inc., 2003).

10. Dr. Caroline Leaf, Who Switched Off My Brain? Controlling Toxic Thoughts and Emotions, rev. ed. (Nashville, TN: Thomas Nelson Publishers, 2009).

11. Ralph Moore, Stress Busters, Kindle edition, (CreateSpace Independent Publishing Platform) 2013.

Chapter 9: Relational Part of the Whole

1. Paul Lee Tan, Encyclopedia of 7700 Illustrations: Signs of The Times, (Thousand Oaks, CA: Assurance Publishers, 1990).

2. Institute of HeartMath, "Emotions Can Change Your DNA," IHM Newsletter, vol. 11, no. 4 (winter 2012), http://www.heartmath.org/templates/ihm/e-newsletter/publication/2012/winter/emotions-can-change-your-dna.php.

3. Institute of HeartMath, "You Can Change Your DNA," IHM Newsletter, vol. 10, no. 2 (summer 2011), http://www.heartmath.org/templates/ihm/e-newsletter/publication/2011/summer/you-can-change-your-dna.php.

4. Chris Crowley and Henry S. Lodge M.D., Younger Next Year: Live Strong, Fit, and Sexy—Until You're 80 And Beyond, Kindle edition, (New York: Workman Publishing Company, Inc., 2007), 270.

5. Ibid, 259.

6. John Bevere, The Bait of Satan: Living Free From the Deadly Trap of Offense, rev. ed. (Lake Mary, FL: Charisma House, 2004), 16.

7. Kevin Dedmon and Chad Dedmon, The Risk Factor: Crossing the Chicken Line Into Your Supernatural Destiny, (Shippensburg, PA: Destiny Image, 2011).

8. Divorcestatistics.info, online article, "Divorce Statistics and Divorce Rate in the USA," 2012, http://www.divorcestatistics.info/divorce-statistics-and-divorce-rate-in-the-usa.html.

9. Rambo, directed by Sylvester Stallone, (2008; Santa Monica, CA: Lionsgate, 2008), DVD.

10. Gladiator, directed by Ridley Scott, (2000; London, UK: Warner Bros, 2003), DVD.

Chapter 10: Financial Part of the Whole

1. Kenneth Ulmer, *Making Your Money Count: Why We Have It, How To Manage It*, (Ventura, CA: Regal Books, 2007), 26, 117.
2. Dave Ramsey, *The Total Money Makeover*, (Nashville, TN: Thomas Nelson, Inc., 2013), 13.
3. Ibid.
4. Kenneth Ulmer, *Making Your Money Count: Why We Have It, How To Manage It*, (Ventura, CA: Regal Books, 2007), 26, 117.
5. Ibid.

Chapter 11: Making the Change

1. *What About Bob?*, directed by Frank Oz, (1991; Burbank, CA: Buena Vista Home Entertainment), DVD.
2. Robert K. Cooper, *The Other 90%: How to Unlock Your Vast Untapped Potential for Leadership and Life*, (New York: Three Rivers Press, 2001).

Chapter 12: Planning Your Life

1. Dean Schabner, "Americans: Overworked, Overstressed," *ABCNews* (online article), http://abcnews.go.com/US/story?id=93604&page=1 (accessed October 5, 2013).
2. Dean Schabner, "Americans Work More Than Anyone," *ABCNews* (online article), http://abcnews.go.com/US/story?id=93364&page=1 (accessed October 5, 2013).
3. Dave Gilson, "Overworked America: 12 Charts That Will Make Your Blood Boil," *MotherJones*, July/August 2011, http://www.motherjones.com/politics/2011/06/speedup-americans-working-harder-charts.
4. John de Graaf and David K. Batker, "Americans Work Too Much for Their Own Good: de Graaf and Batker," *Bloomberg* (online article), November 3, 2011,

http://www.bloomberg.com/news/2011-11-03/americans-work-too-much-for-their-own-good-de-graaf-and-batker.html.

5. Karen Leland and Keith Bailey, *Time Management In An Instant: 60 Ways to Make the Most of Your Day,* Kindle edition (Career Press, Inc., 2008), 19.

6. Brian Tracy, Eat *That Frog!: 21 Great Ways To Stop Procrastinating And Get More Done In Less Time,* 2nd edition, (San Francisco: Berrett-Koehler Publishers, 2007).

7. YouTube, "Timeless Truth from Stephen Covey Put Your Big Rocks in First" https://www.youtube.com/watch?v=F-nxQ9uDdi0 (accessed October 5, 2013).

8. Brian Tracy, Eat *That Frog!: 21 Great Ways To Stop Procrastinating And Get More Done In Less Time,* 2nd edition, (San Francisco: Berrett-Koehler Publishers, 2007).

9. *Mission: Impossible,* Television series, Desilu Productions, Paramount Television, 1966.

10. C. Ray Johnson. *CEO Logic: Hot To Think And Act Like A Chief Executive,* (Career Press, Inc., 1998).

Chapter 13: The Truth About You – and God

1. Joel Osteen, *It's Your Time: Activate Your Faith, Achieve Your Dreams, and Increase in God's Favor,* (New York: Free Press, 2009), 5.

2. Ibid.

Chapter 14: This Never Stops – Keep Climbing

1. *Swiss Family Robinson,* directed by Ken Annakin, (1960; Burbank, CA: Walt Disney Studios Home Entertainment, 2002), DVD.

2. *Indiana Jones,* directed by Steven Spielberg, (1981; Los Angeles, CA: Paramount Pictures, 2008), DVD.

A Note from the Author

Raised by an alcoholic, and a workaholic, I'm a walking miracle. When I was in Jr. High I started taking antidepressants for what is now called IBS (Irritable Bowel Syndrome). I was unaware the doctors were treating me for depression. I have had numerous stress-related diseases including IBS, muscle spasms and cramping (mainly in my back), and even heart arrhythmia a few years ago. Several times I have prayed that I wouldn't die. Now I know these things were all related to my stress levels and how I lived my life.

Other life experiences compelled me to do research and focus on changing my own life so I could live with greatness and excellence. I was tired of living a mediocre life and feeling stressed out! I wanted to enjoy life, and I wanted to enjoy it well into my 80s.

I am 52 years old and probably in the best shape of my life. I enjoy all types of workouts and anything outdoors, especially with other people. I love surfing, bicycling, and going for rides on my Hayabusa with my girlfriend (my wife, Lora). I love eating delicious, wonderfully seasoned, healthy food and watching the sunset, especially at the beach. I am absolutely in love with Jesus, my Savior, and have partnered with Him to bring abundant life to everyone who seeks it.

I invite you to join me on an incredible journey as you elevate every area of your life to live the way God intended you to live...in TOTAL LIFE PURSUIT!

Visit www.TotalLifePursuit.org for more information about the TLP discipleship courses, blog, and more!

25316517R70132

Made in the USA
Charleston, SC
26 December 2013